Child Protective Services

The Globalization of Chaos and Misfortune

Bea Kapinski

LifeRich Publishing is a registered trademark of
The Reader's Digest Association, Inc.

LifeRich Publishing books may be ordered through booksellers or by contacting:

LifeRich Publishing
1663 Liberty Drive
Bloomington, IN 47403
www.liferichpublishing.com
1 (888) 238-8637

ISBN: 978-1-4897-1591-3 (sc)
ISBN: 978-1-4897-1590-6 (hc)
ISBN: 978-1-4897-1592-0 (e)

Library of Congress Control Number: 2018903240

Print information available on the last page.

LifeRich Publishing rev. date: 03/27/2018

I would like to dedicate this book to a wonderful coworker at our Tempe, Arizona, office: Victoria Lopez, a very dedicated worker approximately five years younger than me, who started the job the same time I did, in January 2006. She passed away in June 2016 (several months after I officially retired) from pancreatic cancer.

Victoria was diagnosed approximately a month before her passing; I strongly believe that the demands of the job were a direct cause of her illness. I say this because the whole ten years I knew Victoria, she never had any health issues. She was also a very levelheaded, calm person. Therefore, her lifestyle would have encouraged a much longer and more fruitful number of years if she were not subjected to the kind of stress that our job produces.

I very distinctly remember that in all the years I worked for CPS, I was lucky to go to the doctor every two years for a physical. I was so busy working, and so exhausted when not, that I did not want to take extra time unless an emergency required me to do so. This was likely the same scenario that led to Victoria's untimely demise. Here's to you, Victoria. God bless! We will miss your smile, cheerfulness, and kindness always. I intend to donate a portion of the proceeds from this book to Victoria's family; she left behind a daughter and baby grandchild.

Contents

Introduction

While I like to help people, I am far from being self-sacrificing or a crusader for causes. Nor do I care to be political in any sense. I believe, after working for Child Protective Services (CPS) as a case manager for ten years, that the major way to affect change for CPS children and families is through education. Education is linked directly to resources, because the education I am referring to is not necessarily school per se but rather education regarding child abuse and its origins. As an agency, we must examine those factors that contribute to child abuse. Then we need to strategize and change, or even alleviate, the elements that comprise this abuse as much as possible.

We need to do this by providing the resources and the tools to fight the cycles of abuse. The resources and tools I refer to involve therapy and therapy-based services. The elements of domestic violence and physical, emotional, and sexual abuse have components of conditioning and beliefs held by human beings that need to be changed. The need to understand these elements comes first before behavior modification and change can take effect.

The alternative to not reaching out to CPS parents and helping to work with and educate them mean more cases like the ones portrayed in this book, more removals of children and more severances granted, more children subjected to child abuse, more breakdowns in family units, more horror stories in the making. And while I don't purport to have the answers needed to succeed at this enormous undertaking, the key to attainment of those answers in general is through a systematic approach, with schools of social work teaming up with legislatures to devise flexible but consistent budgets with which to meet the needs of the types of CPS families we serve. How as a society are we going to provide these services if the means to do so are not in our state budgets, especially if legislators continue to skirt around the issues without understanding what those issues are or their results? And if we are not committed to doing this, the situation will continue to grow larger, as will the expense. Cutting corners is definitely not the answer. Nor is ignoring the cause and effect that we have witnessed over time in case history studies.

The base of much of the worst child abuse we witness stems from addiction, whether from alcohol or drugs, both prescribed and illegal. Poverty and untreated mental health issues are also factors.

One of the disturbing questions is why is this trend of CPS involvement becoming worse and more prevalent through time? (We have quite a few more dependencies and severances here in Arizona now than when I started ten years ago.) Why do we have such a lack of success in addressing CPS families effectively?

The answer in part is that the legislature cut social services, including contracted agencies such as Family Builders and Family Connections that previously stepped in and worked actively with CPS families to help resolve or assist families with their problems. These agencies served as a valuable safety net and were the eyes and ears for our families and their needs. It is a vicious circle; cutting services creates more expensive messes down the road. Top administrators, who don't see this picture or don't acknowledge it, are being paid big money, while the little case worker sees this all too clearly, each case's development and history. The multitude of cases keep increasing, both in number and severity.

While I feel illegal immigration has contributed to the problem in the quantity of CPS children and the costs associated with our department's involvement, at this point it is more important to focus on answers. In general, we need to not only educate parents but hold them more accountable for their actions. I refer specifically but not exclusively to drugs. By comparison, nobody hesitates to hold the CPS worker accountable when something goes wrong on a case, but why do we allow, for example, drug moms to continue to give birth to substance-exposed newborns (SEN)—in other words, mothers who use drugs while pregnant—without any repercussions? (Although the agency substantiates on their CPS report for SEN, the substantiation of the report is more a formality than enforcing consequences.)

Why can't we change the law and incarcerate these particular moms for their crime of exposing a fetus to drugs, if not for the first baby, then at least for baby number two and so on? An SEN baby can grow up with all kinds of medical and physical effects. Where are the infants' rights? Incarceration cost money, but the mom would be forced to participate in a substance abuse program. Sadly, most addicts will not willingly go through a drug program if given the choice but will generally continue to have children nonetheless. Wouldn't education and consequences lessen the chances of future SEN babies being born? In that case, incarceration would cost less than a child living in the foster care system for eighteen years and potentially suffering medical conditions due to drug exposure. Medical treatment also costs a lot of money.

Most people, including addicts, do not desire to be incarcerated as a punishment. If a drug mom can walk away freely from the mess she has created, she will continue to create the same mess until she is stopped or forced to change by being held accountable.

If an illegal immigrant has an SEN child, then deportation should be a threat to the mother if the mother has a criminal history. If she were held accountable for her actions, she might not be so quick to use drugs or keep having babies in Arizona. Most of the illegal immigrants love their children, so that would give them good motivation not to use substances. (Also to be considered is that many CPS moms are impregnated before their current CPS case is over, even when the case is heading for severance.)

These are a few considerations and keys to finding answers. Now comes the story: a history of cases that this author has personally worked, raw and chilling and most of them hopeless. Anybody who is a student of social work should be required to read this type of book, not because it is a masterpiece, not because it is inspiring, not because it contains great wisdom, but because it is an honest and revealing account of the work involved and a warning about the depths of depravity that exist in child abuse cases. It also shows the CPS worker's vulnerability, which should be factored in, as well as the political elements that intersect. (To my knowledge, this is the only book ever written from the CPS worker's point of view.)

What we need are enlightened young social workers who can actively step into the arena of CPS, schools, and hospitals with a greater quest to pursue and develop individualized answers for children suffering child abuse, rather than just rely on simple textbook phrases to deal with it. The corresponding goals need to be child and parent services–based to encourage the growth of the family's well-being, to help these struggling families identify and utilize family-based strengths so they have a chance to succeed in both society and the world within. At least they might possibly be made aware of where they stand in order to move forward, on the right foot.

1

My History Leading Up to CPS / Department of Child Services (DCS)

I always thought that a book about Child Protective Services would make for interesting reading, especially one written by a worker. There is much mystique and misunderstanding about CPS, to put it mildly. Before I became an employee with Child Protective Services, I would hear in the news, from time to time, about CPS cases that blew up. I felt blessed not to be born into a sordid world of chaos and CPS.

When my own parents died, I felt lost to the world. I have always had a strong bond with family. That was just the way I was raised, so I knew no other way. Unfortunately, my parents did not live to ripe old ages; some parents reach their eighties and nineties. When my parents died, it was like being a teenager all over again: I felt uncertain about my future, my fate, family, and friends, even day-to-day living. And I was forty years old when Mom died. It was just me and the gulf of alienation surrounding me on all sides—and I was an island, standing alone. Although I have a sibling, we lived many miles apart at that time. So that relationship was not helpful at all. I never realized the loss of my parents would be as great as it was, even though I can still hear my mom saying, "You'll miss me when I'm gone." That understatement could have easily swallowed me up and spat me out.

After my dad passed away and both parents were gone, I decided to move far away from Florida. I had moved there to be closer to my parents. But now I wanted to move away from the memories, from the pain, from the new emptiness I had found and wanted to lose so desperately. While a person can never truly run away from his or her troubles, I still wanted to try. Although in my younger years my parents and I had our fair share of quarrels, I wound up moving to Florida to be near them after they retired. As I got older, I was more on their wavelength, more comfortable with them, and happier with our relationship than I had ever been. Having family was indeed grand. I could finally appreciate it. But now my folks were gone for all eternity. I obtained a divorce from my nice husband, who worked too many hours and was too quiet. He did not have a clue about the depths of my despair; nor did he attempt to uncover those depths. For once, I was at a loss for words to express the emptiness that suddenly plagued me. I felt like a robot, withholding feelings, disconnected from the world but going through the motions.

The night my mom died, it was my own little sweet boy who felt my pain and acknowledged it as I lay down next to him (a ritual I performed every night to encourage him to sleep; I joyfully cherished this ritual, as my husband always worked late) and waited, sobbing uncontrollably, for him to fall asleep. This beautiful little toddler, with his dark hair and dark eyes, long eyelashes, tiny nose, white baby skin, and short but thick little hands, solemnly declared in his sweet, baby voice, "Do not cry, Mama. I love you." That was the only comfort I was to know for quite some time: that and the comfort of God. I learned of God in mysterious ways, and when I needed Him the most, He was there, plain and simple.

At the time Mom died, I started going to religious services. I still felt empty, but among my tears was some solace. I can't quite explain it, but I knew that I felt a little ray of light burning in my soul, drawing me along like a magnet. This sensation brought me hope that sustained me, for grief is a stranger in the dark: weary and leery, always uncomfortable to his visitor, a stranger visited by emptiness or despair who is all-consuming but never quite welcomed by anyone. (Gee, was this my prelude to CPS? It sure sounds like a description of how many people perceive us CPS workers!)

I was keenly aware of another thing at the time of my parents' death: I felt or noticed my friends becoming distant; they could find no words to comfort me, so they sought not to even try. I did not blame them. I knew they cared but lacked the proper insight or tools with which to comfort me. So I put forth more effort to compensate. I took classes at my temple; I thought the structure and lessons would bring me the understanding I needed to get through it all. I felt praying was the appropriate response to the death of one's parents. This I believed and still do. In addition, I believed wholeheartedly that God is the eternal parent of the entire human race, no matter what religion one follows: God is the common denominator and multiplier of life, He who brings us together and apart. Maybe that is grace—or part of it.

At the time my dad died, I was walking on thin ice mentally. Once a reasonably happy, upbeat person, I now felt on the borderline of suicidal. For wasn't my parents' identity really mine? It was scary. Even when my physician prescribed meds for me, I gave up immediately on them. They dulled the pain, but the pain did not cease. And prayer helped, but not 24-7.

Right around the time that Daddy died, a beautiful neighbor in her late twenties or early thirties, with two young children and a husband, had done what I had only contemplated; she killed herself in a gruesome manner. She jumped in front of the train as it was coming into our local Pembroke Pines, Florida, train station. I thought perhaps her husband had left her for another woman. I came to find out that her own parents had died recently in an accident, and she was so despondent she did not know what else to do. The only difference I could see between her and me was that she had acted upon her thoughts, whereas I had not. Unfortunately, she could not take back the impulse that led to her untimely demise. I never knew this woman's name, but I remembered seeing her walking her child to school. I would also walk my son to school every morning; they attended the same elementary school. This woman lived across the street from us, and we were both a block or so away from the school. It was horribly tragic, to say the least.

My dad's dying and this woman's suicide happened around the time that Princess Diana died in a car crash. I felt the whole world had gone mad. Because my neighbor felt the kind of despair I felt, I mourned for her in my heart for a long time. I wanted to go over to her family's house with food and apologies, but, not knowing them, I felt it was inappropriate. I did not have the right words to use either, so I just couldn't do it. Still, I harbored it in my thoughts for a long time. Finally, the suicidal stranger was the person who snapped me back to reality.

I sought temporary grief counseling through the hospice where my dad had stayed before he died. I also volunteered to help children through my temple. I went to a nursery school in a low-income area one or two days a week and read to the children. I did volunteer work at my son's grade school. I taught yoga at a homeless shelter and mentored a client there. I went to graduate school and received a master's degree in humanities. All this helped me maintain but not enough for me to stay put. I was restless and lost. So I moved far away.

But these factors comprised some of the background that led up to my days with CPS. I remember how good it felt helping the less fortunate when I did volunteer work. For example, although I had taught yoga many years (at a school and several gyms), the thank yous I received from the homeless population sounded more sincere than those of my other, regular patrons who paid for their lessons and sometimes appeared at class, perhaps mindlessly or out of habit more than necessity. Or maybe the appreciation from the homeless population was more notable because the homeless had salvaged so little in the course of being homeless, or maybe because they salvaged so much—mentally, not materially. In any case, yoga is a great stress reducer, and I cannot imagine anything more stressful than being homeless—or losing someone you love to death, either.

This was, as I said, the prelude to my CPS days.

2

Linda Walker

I started my job with CPS six years after my dad had died. I had moved from Florida to Nevada to Arizona during that time. One of my first cases was an about-to-be homeless woman who called in a CPS report on herself because she was desperate about what to do. Linda Walker had six kids—can you imagine what a person in her shoes might be thinking? I am glad if you can imagine it, because I could not begin to. I met Linda in an undesirable part of Phoenix at the Motel 6 where she and her family were staying. Linda explained that they were on their last paid night at the motel.

"Can you please do something?" Linda pleaded with me quietly in an undemanding tone of voice.

I went back to the CPS office I was assigned to and made calls to all the local shelters. Naturally, nobody had any availability to accommodate a family of seven. That would have been too easy. Nothing in CPS was ever easy: not the work, not the people, not the policies, not the outcomes.

Anyway, I stuck my neck out and notified Motel 6 that I was with CPS and said that we would foot the bill. "Let her stay the night." I knew no such thing to be true. But I figured, the worse that can happen is that I might have to cover the sixty dollars for them to spend the night out of my own pocket. How symbolic that was, transpiring at a time when I was losing my own house.

I could not afford to keep the house any longer. (I had entered a relationship that left me holding the bag and could not afford the big mortgage alone—probably why I have experienced few trusting relationships.) But thankfully I did not lose my house to foreclosure. I was able to put the house on the market and sell it. Prices were plummeting, but I still made a very modest profit. That was the only house I had ever owned up to that time.

I was certainly brought up middle-class. I went on trips all over the US and to parts of Europe, went out to many nightclubs and decent restaurants, belonged to a country club with my family as a child, had several cars bought for me by my parents, had beautiful diamond rings (the big ones my mom left me and the smaller ones I bought myself). A first cousin is a movie star, another first cousin a major surgeon, yet another first cousin a lawyer and an accountant. A second or third cousin is a professional artist; several second and third cousins were successful engineers; two cousins were CEOs of companies. Even though I have worn fancy, expensive clothes to swank affairs, have drank good champagne, ridden in limos, seen pro baseball, basketball, and football games (go, Packs, go), though I have done charity work, as my mother did before me, and I finished college with a 3.5 average, nonetheless I have also known hard times. I've seen and felt less affluence, as well as too much of it, compared to the way I was raised. I am a perfect example of someone who has been on both sides of the track. That has helped tremendously in my insight into the social work capacity I possess. I would say the biggest reason for my lack of prosperity was being single and having to do it all on my own at a certain point, with no outside help. Nobody can ever accuse me of sitting on my fat ass, being waited on hand and foot, making sure my nails are always perfect while I trivialize others hardships in the pursuit of frivolous existence. I was too busy merely trying to survive in middle age when it came right down to it, working a rather hard-core job for umpteen hours a week. (I hope I don't sound bitter. I am grateful instead, because it did give me a real purpose, no matter how difficult it was.)

That was the reason I stuck my neck out for Linda, one of my earliest cases. Surely I would want someone to show me the same compassion if I were in her shoes. It was no wonder that at least half of my clients commended me for being so caring. Some of them acted like I was the last real human being who worked for CPS. "Oh, you answer your phone. Nobody else does!" (Really? That is part of the job.) "I have finally met someone who listens and helps try to solve or assist me with my concerns." It never amazed me to hear such stuff. Hey, I was just trying to do my job! (Maybe they were pulling my leg?) Hearing appreciation from strangers in need was good fortune returned, and those needs varied to an extreme sometimes.

I wanted to sleep at night, no matter how few hours were afforded me, with a clear conscience.

The situation involving Linda worked out well. By nature, when it comes to my work, I have proven to be quick and full of initiative. I put in for services for Linda with Family Connections, immediately. Family Connections stepped in fast to assist. Those were better days for CPS in Arizona, when there were more services accessible to help avoid filing so many dependencies. ("Filing a dependency" means a child or children have to be removed from their home and go through foster care and the court system.) This number has grown and grown in Arizona, and it is shocking the administrators have never analyzed the connection; they cut important services in the attempt to save a few bucks. In doing so, they have cost the taxpayers thousands extra with the greater number of dependencies that have had to be filed. They did not identify the importance of the correlation between Family Builders and Family Connections, which were our major contracted services, and how their services helped prevent removals. Please keep in mind that no children on my cases ever died, and the services helped enormously, but if not, a dependency would then become the next step in the process.

My provider indeed stepped up to the plate; their agency took over paying the nightly rent at the Motel 6 and made it retroactive. Whew! No extra money out of my pocket that I could hardly afford.

Then there came the day when Family Connections was going to help secure a house for Linda. I am not sure who was more excited, her or me. But I got a call from the provider, telling me suddenly that they could not help Linda any longer. I asked them why. The reply astounded me. (After I'd worked with CPS for much longer, nothing came to surprise me too much, but the beginning was a different story.)

The reply was that Linda was going to let her boyfriend move in with her, that she wouldn't give him up. Therefore, they weren't going to help her anymore. I told the provider to please hold off. "Let me talk to Linda." I called and left Linda a message, and she called back. I immediately proceeded to lecture the young mom. "You know, Linda, I had no idea about this boyfriend moving in with you. Family Connections won't help you if you let him do so. And what does he contribute anyway? Is he just dead weight? Because at least Tom really cares about you and the kids, and he works and wants to do something for you." (Tom was father of several of the younger children. He had gotten out of prison recently and made a vow to me that he wanted to stay on the straight and narrow and do the right thing. "Good. Yes. Go for it, Tom!")

I told her, "That's a sign of love. A guy who is there for a free ride is just a user. You have it hard, and you don't need anyone else using you or making your life any harder than it already is, Linda. Haven't you been used enough?"

I went on and on, not yelling, not mean, just matter-of-fact and extremely long-winded (anyone who truly knows me can vouch for that about me; when the mood takes over, watch out. I won't bother coming up for air.) During this discourse, I was waiting for and expecting Linda to just hang up on me, detached. I figured after a while she would have enough and slam the phone down without a word, or angrily use a few choice cuss words first. I imagined she would reply, "Why, how dare you? Who do you think you are to tell me what to do?"

As I went on and on, I was wondering if Linda had put the phone down silently and wasn't listening anymore. But it was none of those things. To my amazement when she finally spoke, Linda was actually thanking me. She said, "Bea, I never had the kind of mother who would or could offer the kind of insight, advice, and encouragement you have offered me."

I was so shocked that my only reply was, "Really?"

Linda went on to tell me her background: how her own mom lost her kids, including Linda, to CPS. Her maternal grandmother was very irresponsible and self-absorbed. Nonetheless, it hurt and scared Linda immensely. Linda's mom was apparently never able to focus on Linda and her siblings. The outcome was that Linda was put into the foster care system.

She went to a very nice foster home. Linda was somewhere between the ages of nine and eleven at the time. Linda said the people were nice and lived in a nice home, but they were also very strict. Linda felt very pressured, especially with all the thoughts and feelings related to her mother fresh on her mind. Though Linda was a straight A student in school, she had trouble focusing on school. Then she wound up rebelling and running off when she was about fourteen or fifteen. To top it all off, she became pregnant. She tried to return to the foster home, but they wouldn't accept her back, so she proceeded on the road she was on. She moved from one relationship to another; she was very fragile emotionally, and apparently the men she chose were not ideal companions, to put it diplomatically.

Linda felt very bad that the foster parents would not forgive her and give her another chance, and she said that deep down inside she truly appreciated and cared about them. It made Linda develop a self-loathing attitude. After she was on her own for a while, Linda's biological mom drifted back into the picture, trying to take advantage of Linda. Linda's mom stayed for free with Linda, getting whatever she could out of the arrangement.

I had met Linda's mom in the middle of it all. Unlike pretty Linda, with her nice features and well-kept, medium-length brown hair, nice skin, cute figure, and acceptable clothing, Linda's mom was a short, almost skeletal, almost bald woman (maybe she'd taken to meth or hard liquor, I surmised), mostly toothless, with horrible skin. Linda was not yet thirty; her mother could barely be sixty and didn't look a day over seventy or eighty.

That was one of my internal jokes from the meth class we took. People who use hard drugs, in particular methamphetamine, the killer cheap man's drug, will age at an alarming rate. The teeth become elongated; users become skinny and horrid-looking, with very bad skin. Hard-core meth freaks usually have open sores all over their faces and continually scratch and pick at them. Yuck!

And the drug does not just take a toll on a person's body. It literally eats away at a person's brain and can make the person insane as they continue to use meth. Hence, on meth, it is not uncommon to experience hallucinations. During bad hallucinations, parents have even bludgeoned their children to death, thinking God told them to sacrifice the child. Please. Let's not give the credit to God. It was the devil of all chaos and horror that made those parents on meth commit unspeakable acts on their kids. Some people call the devil Satan; a CPS worker like me probably would call the devil meth. To top it off, meth is a very addictive drug.

Anyway, I told Linda, who was not into drugs or alcohol, who swore she wanted to be the good person her mother was not, that she was indeed smart and admirable. I said Linda should maybe consider going back to school to try to resume her straight-A average and get herself into a good profession. That would give her independence and confidence. That way she could set a great example for her kids, who were not abused and did love her dearly. And Linda thanked me again and proclaimed that nobody had ever given her encouragement before or spent an hour on the phone with her like I had, having a heart-to-heart conversation. She said how much she'd needed that, how much she'd wanted that from someone. (I was more than happy to oblige.)

When Family Connections called me the next day, they said, "I don't know what you said to Linda, but she has done a 100 percent turnaround. She dumped the boyfriend. She's willing to do everything the right way, and we're getting her moved into her new place next week." I was elated to hear this latest development! It did my soul a lot of good. Can you imagine the "luck" I had to have someone like Linda as my first client, to start out with a real success story in the making, someone who gave me hope in mankind? For some reason, it reminded me of a few lines from a Moody Blues song of old: "And when you stop and think about it, you won't believe it's true, that all the loving you've been giving has all been meant for you."

Whatever I had given Linda was what Linda had given me—hope for something better. It wasn't just Linda either; it was also the father, Tom, who decided to turn over a new leaf after his incarceration. I remember I had received a voice message from Tom, probably the most memorable message I had ever received from anyone, ever. And it did not sound like just hype, either. It sounded genuine and caring. It made me feel proud of this man, whom I'd never even met. Tom stated very passionately, definitely bordering on the dramatic, how he loved Linda, his kids, and Linda's other kids. He said he regretted doing wrong and going to prison and said he wanted to make good. I was very touched by his message; it moved me deeply. I prayed that Tom would do just that: work hard, prosper, stay on the straight and narrow, and reap all the benefits, not only for himself but also for his family. Nobody ever knows where a person's intentions will take that person, but hopefully Tom was able to maintain his vision to the end.

I know a case like Linda's was one of those fine few definitive cases where you as the worker just loved the outcome, the way it played out, the win-win team situation that you were so blessed to be part of. How very rare indeed that was. I found out over and over, sadly, how very rare indeed that was. (I also use the criteria that Linda's case was successful because I did not receive any further CPS reports on her.)

3

The Applebys, CPS Training, and Bits and Pieces of the Past

The next case I had was a dependency. The dad was rushed to the hospital. His name was Henry Powell. He stayed in a state of limbo for one or two weeks. They did not know whether he would live or not. Henry's girls, Stacey and Melinda, were approximately twelve and fourteen years old.

The stepmom, who had left Henry after five years of marriage, was still a part of the scenario. Henry and the stepmom had been divorced maybe a year or less. Sally was her name. When she found out what happened to Henry, she immediately rushed over to check on the girls. Sally thought, based upon the girls' behavior and whatever clues she picked up on, that at the time the girls were high on drugs. I was unsure if her involvement was because she cared about the girls or if she was trying to butt in.

I did want to take proper precaution. The girls were taken via Rapid Response assessments to be drug tested. Sure enough, when the test results came back, they tested positive for both marijuana and meth. Wonderful. The girls claimed they had smoked marijuana and that it must have been laced with meth. To be quite honest, I was too naïve to know if that was possible or not. However, I followed my gut and assumed the worst. Doing our job, we learn to be skeptical, because most CPS workers feel we are constantly being handed stories by kids and adults. Most of the time it turns out to be true, unfortunately.

In any case, the girls were temporarily put in a group home. I was very touched, drugs or no drugs, by the girls' apparent devotion to their ill father. They appeared worried sick and very stressed over what the outcome of Henry's plight would be.

Then, suddenly, as hard as his illness had taken Henry, he made a miraculous and sudden recovery. He still had a way to go before he was in the clear. During that time, Henry confided to me that the girls' mother had gotten into drugs when Melinda and Stacey were quite young. Henry overlooked it until he could do so no longer; then he gave their mom an ultimatum. It was time to choose either the girls and family or drugs. So Mom chose drugs and never looked back.

It was one of several heartbreaks that Henry was subjected to. After their mom left, Henry met the stepmom, Sally, at church. Henry liked Sally's values, and they wound up getting married after going together for a period of time. Henry was happy; now he had someone to help raise his girls.

It was hard for Stacey and Melinda to adjust, however, after losing their mom and now having a stepmom in the picture. While Sally had good values, she was strict and inflexible. Naturally, the girls acted out; they rebelled. One day Sally decided she had had enough and called it quits. More heartbreak for Henry. It was a progression of events. Sally and the girls kept clashing about everything: the way they dressed, the things they did, the friends they had, the music they played. They clashed and clashed until they could clash no more. Nobody was willing to compromise.

I personally felt that the more mature party, meaning the adult, should have sought compromise. But those are my own beliefs. Maybe that is easier said than done. Sally had her reasons why she stood steadfast in her ways, though I can't recall what they were. I think they had something to do with her own son taking a turn for the worse in his young adulthood or something to do with Sally's dad being rigid. The girls did try on their part, I believe in my heart, to get along with Sally, if for no other reason than they knew she made their dad happy.

Watching them together, Henry and Sally looked like they were a cute couple, until you heard about all their bad history together. Henry was short and thin and had nice features and sharp blue eyes. Sally had very pretty hair, thick and stylish, and pretty eyes and teeth. Sally dressed smartly. Henry was soft spoken and gentlemanly. So much for looks being deceiving.

One hot summer day, around 120 degrees, after his electricity had been turned off for nonpayment, while the girls were visiting him, we were roasting in his living room. It did not surprise me when Henry told me that he was from a very middle-class family. Even though Henry did not have money, his manners revealed that fact. The girls were equally polite and well mannered. They always used the words *please* and *thank you*, as if that was second nature to them. In the way they carried themselves and in their general demeanor, they acted like young girls who were used to the best of everything. Their vocabulary reflected that as well.

His two girls were beautiful. Stacey had blonde hair and big brown eyes. She was as sweet a girl as one could find: mature, helpful to her dad. She was very short and had a pixie quality about her. Sister Melinda had long black hair, was more average in height, and very striking. The girls were way too skinny, probably from the meth, but they dressed in adorable clothes and knew how to do their hair better than I ever could, as well as apply their makeup like professionals.

In the midst of all the turmoil, Sally told me that she was going to remarry Henry. Sally's manner was very abrupt. It is possible Sally's dad had been a military man. Sally presented herself that way. Her statement sounded more like an order than a well-thought-out decision agreed upon by the family members. In the end, Sally up and disappeared, her total instability leaving Henry sad and exasperated. Apparently, when Sally had re-entered the picture, she had stayed temporarily with some other man because she only received a limited monthly check. I try hard not to be prejudicial, but looking at the situation and Sally, I concluded to myself that it was very CPS in every chaotic, inconsistent detail.

When the case went to court, I suggested to the attorney assigned to the case by the attorney general's office that Stacey should be allowed to go home; Melinda should be kept in foster care because Melinda was the child at risk. Both girls had been AWOL, but Stacey had returned right away. Melinda always influenced Stacey in undesirable ways. Melinda was the older sister who turned Stacey on to meth. Stacey was just playing follow the leader and trying to avoid conflict. She was the pleaser. The main problem with Stacey was that she was always busy trying to please everyone.

Stacey was the person who most resembled her father. She was a bit on the weak side but definitely far from bad when one considered her motivations for doing some of the things she did. It came out after a period of time that Melinda was all about Melinda and only Melinda. Melinda didn't care whom she did or didn't please. Initially Melinda tried to disguise that fact, with ulterior motives.

The attorney snapped at me when I suggested that we split the case, with Stacey going home and Melinda staying in CPS care. "You can't do it that way!" (Oh, please, I only work here. What do I know?) My attorney nearly shouted at me. "Didn't they train you?"

I replied rather neutrally, "Well, let's see. We go through about three months of training. I think they might have covered that part in about fifteen seconds."

That might have even been an understatement. When we were hired, the state of Arizona sent new workers to what is called CORE training, I am unsure however, what CORE stands for. The CORE training institute was located near downtown. There was a large group of us. We had around three months' worth of training crammed into us Monday through Friday from approximately nine to four. They covered social work, court, the computer, policy, investigation interviewing techniques, child-safety assessments, cultural diversity, and so on. We had not stacks but boxes full of paperwork by the time the classes ended.

Graduate school literature classes didn't even compete in the amount of material we covered, and in my grad school literature class, I was required to read thirteen books in one semester! It is understandable why one must have a college degree to be accepted into CPS. The discipline needed to cover the material would probably be a mind blower for a nonscholastic type of person. Though I had always considered myself a good student, averaging almost B+ through high school and even through graduate school without having to study excessively, I felt like I had amnesia by the time I finished CORE training.

The social work courses were good, though, and gave me great insight into things I'd never considered: how hard it is for a child to be removed from his or her home and life that child knew, even when there has been abuse going on. A child clings to what he or she knows. A lot of times siblings will be very close, due to the nature of the abuse that occurs. If siblings are sometimes unavoidably separated just like that, can we even begin to imagine the trauma and loss that child experiences? Studies from the '70s and '80s point to the fact that many children who suffered abuse and/or were removed from their homes turned to crime when they came of age. Sometimes they would start even earlier.

That is why the newer CPS ideology removes kids as a last resort instead of as an end-all remedy (depending on the current director of the agency, in some cases). Overall, our agency tries to or should provide significant services to help the parent or parents cope and, in some cases, learn effective, alternative methods of child rearing that can keep children safe. It seems the majority of CPS parents do experience more trouble coping and developing coping skills to deal with life stressors, which is crucially relevant.

If, however, the parent or parents refuse to engage in services or do not take services seriously by completing the requirements and showing improvement in important areas concerning abuse, our agency would then contemplate severance of rights. Of course, that process goes before the judge. There are standard time frames for the person to exhibit substantial, significant, consistent changes in behavior patterns, usually up to two years

One of the parts of our CORE training I remember most clearly was the film about the nanny cam. It was a true story that involved a mom who hired a babysitter **for** her child, approximately ten months old. One day the mom noticed a bruise on the baby's head. She asked the sitter about it the next day. The sitter replied that the baby had not gotten the bruise at the sitter's house; it must have happened at home. The mom had a surprising and interesting reaction.

She requested if she could leave a camcorder to be used if the sitter were leaving the house. (The sitter's husband was there during the day, so periodically the sitter would leave to run an errand while her husband would temporarily babysit in her absence.) The sitter responded that if she were running out, she would turn the recorder on until she got back. Apparently, and thankfully, she didn't tell her husband.

It might have been the same day or the next day when it happened. What the sitter saw when she came back, she could hardly believe. The uncensored segment of the film they showed us in class showed the baby in a playpen. The sitter's husband came into the room. At first he spoke in a sweet voice, saying, "Hi, baby, how are you?" That kind of thing.

Then the next thing we saw, and there was no waste of time to add to the horror, the man picked up the baby and flung her across the room! She landed. He went over to her using a sweet voice. She was half crying but stopped. The baby must have been terrified. The man proceeded to punch her and shake her. Then he dropped or threw her back in the playpen. Upon seeing this footage, the woman called the police. They arrested the sitter's husband. He spent way too little time in jail, maybe several years or so. But the point was all the abuse left only a tiny bruise on the baby.

When investigators conduct interviews, we are very concerned about bruises on babies. Babies do not bruise easily, as is evident in the nanny cam tape. (Little children are another story.)

The other most memorable part from CORE was the story of a shaken baby. They interviewed a young mom who had a baby with an ex-boyfriend. The two parents shared the baby back and forth so that both parents could spend time with the baby. It was thought or implied that the boyfriend had not been in favor of the breakup, but did he have to kill the baby over that fact? Apparently he felt he did, because that was exactly what happened.

I forget the age of the baby, but they taped his confession. He claimed he only shook the baby a little. Forensics has studied shaken-baby syndrome and can determine how long and how hard a baby was shaken. They determined the father must have shaken the baby for twenty seconds. It did not take long to cause the baby's death. Why? Because babies' heads are very sensitive and not yet formed. It was a very tragic tale of a yet another young person making a poor choice. Any teen having a baby should enroll in mandatory classes to hopefully avoid these type of situations.

There has been much child abuse over the years. I remember crying when I still lived in Florida when I heard about a two-year-old who was beaten to death by his parents for wetting his pants. I don't think they were young teen parents, but it was a tragedy just the same. That child had been placed in foster care, but when the parents completed services, the child was given back. Everyone blames CPS that the child was returned, but the human element can be unpredictable sometimes.

CPS workers are not supplied with crystal balls to predict the future or how parents will react to children's errors. I can't even imagine how angry a person could become just over a soiled diaper. I don't remember the rest of that sad story; it was not one of my cases.

Returning to the situation with Stacey and Melinda, my attorney probably understood the truth of my statement about splitting the case. Whether she did or not, I was surprised that the court ordered just what I'd recommended; they released Stacey to Dad, and Melinda stayed in the group home until she finally went AWOL permanently. That did not take long either.

I ran into that attorney at our Glendale office about a year or so later, and she said to me, "Don't I remember you from a case?"

"Sure," I replied. I smiled. "But I would rather not get into it." Sarcasm works well with attorneys, at least with the CPS attorneys I worked with. That attorney might have even been the same attorney who trained us on our legal training. It is so easy to forget things, especially when one works for CPS, where there is so much to remember all the time, including things that you wish you could just forget.

I wound up transferring Stacey from the group home to her dad's. The case had already been transferred to the ongoing unit, but nobody from ongoing was responding when everyone at court wanted to know the status as to when Stacey would return home. I thought I was doing a favor by delivering Stacey to her dad's house. Guess again. Instead of being thanked, I started receiving emails questioning why I was the one who returned Stacey. (Because nobody else would? Because nobody answered my emails?)

At that point, I had to be on the defensive. I advised my interrogator that I had sent several inquiries at least about the arrangements; nobody in ongoing, supervisor or case manager, had as much as replied to me. I was hard-pressed for what to do. Being a new employee, I felt it was okay to return the child once it was agreed upon at court. I didn't want to defy a court order and get in trouble for that! The outcome was rather comical. First I was criticized for taking the action that I took. The same supervisor who interrogated me later gave me a special recognition award for taking the initiative to follow through and help their unit by returning Stacey! Go figure, right? CPS is so laden with stressful situations that this kind of occurrence is more likely than not. One minute you are chastised; the next minute you are praised for virtually the same thing.

After Stacey had been with her dad for a while, she and Henry stopped by our office one night when I was working late, which was most nights, to say hi. Henry asked if I wanted to go out for coffee sometime, but I told him that we were forbidden by policy to date or have social contact with anyone involved in a CPS case. Henry said he understood. It made me feel bad, in the sense I did feel very attached to his lovely girls. I realize how hard going through the majority of their life without a real mother figure must have been for the girls. I can't say that Sally fit that role, though she tried.

When I was young, maybe nine, there was a girl in our neighborhood who was my sister's age, about twelve. Her name was Michelle. Michelle's mother was murdered in cold blood one day. That was before days of heavy crime. We lived in a modest middle-class neighborhood. Nonetheless, one day the doorbell rang, so the story goes. Michelle's mother went to answer the door, and someone gunned her down, as if it were nothing.

Michelle came home from school and found the body. Naturally, she started having trouble in school. Michelle was in a girl scout troop with my sister; our mother was the scout leader. My mom tried using firm love, I guess you would call it, but Michelle was too messed up to snap out of it. Michelle wound up going down the wrong path. She got into trouble and didn't care a bit. All I could think while the situation was transpiring was *Poor Michelle*. I didn't blame her a bit for her behavior. I could not even imagine how devastated I would be if that had been me instead of her. Michelle was an only child, which made the situation worse.

I don't know more about the sad ending to the sad story of Michelle. I pray that a decent, effective social worker in the state of Wisconsin (where I was born and raised and where this occurred) was able to administer to Michelle's needs and help her heal through the horrible fate that fell upon her and her father. I never heard more after Michelle initially got into trouble, so hopefully that was a good sign. I don't remember my sister mentioning Michelle again, so it is possible that she and her dad moved elsewhere.

We are products of our environments, and the element of fate does come into play, like with Michelle and her family. When I was five years old, an older bully came up to me on the street as I was walking home from school. He grabbed me when nobody was around, held a knife to my throat, and called me a kike. And he said if I told, he would kill me. What did I do? I kept my religion a secret until I was an older adult, though most people probably knew anyway. It was not the most rational reaction on my part but the aftereffect of fate based upon my age and circumstances. At least the bully didn't kill me or threaten me anymore. Talking about things can be very liberating, I learned down the road.

I peeked into Henry's case over a year, closer to two years, after I was finished with the case. I believe that Melinda was still AWOL, perhaps following in her mother's drug-habit footsteps? Stacey and her dad stuck together like glue, but times were not easy. Henry, due to poor health, had limited work options, and, therefore, money was also limited. They continued to have financial troubles after Henry lost the job he had been at for so many years.

On the bright side, Henry was still alive, and Stacey was there, hanging in with her dad. Stacey was a bright girl with good grades. Maybe Stacey would be able to help her poor dad out when she became an adult. I bet that she would if she could. And at least the dependency was dismissed and CPS was out of their lives. Hooray. Two points for them!

4

The Case of the Halbrooks: Aspects of our Job

Not long after my first Henry case, I had a case involving another Henry, plus his wife Elsa and their six kids. They had had a bunch of prior CPS experiences. I noted that the reports seemed to center around one child, Katie. I went out to their little house; it was horrendously filthy. That was what the report centered around. The place looked like it had not been cleaned in years. I am not just talking about dust and needing a quick sweep or mop. Dirt was caked on like oil wherever I looked. There were also piles of debris all over the place.

Katie was around thirteen when I first met her. One or two of Katie's siblings were adults and did not live in the Phoenix area. Katie came across as quiet and sweet, as did her siblings. When I arrived at the residence, all family members present smiled, and I purposely made myself out to be very friendly and congenial—until it was time for me to leave. I told the parents, "I don't know what's wrong here. I can't find anything too bad, except the condition of this house. Nonetheless, if I receive one more CPS report on this family, I will have to remove your children. So if there are any problems, think of calling me first, and let me try to assist you."

After I made it crystal clear that this was a promise, not a threat, I enlisted the help of our provider, Family Preservation, to step in and try to determine what needed to be addressed. One possible concern was that the children were being homeschooled. The lessons were at a second grade level. Because the kids' ages ranged between ten and seventeen, I was very alarmed, to put it mildly. I called the homeschooling board, but we only danced around the issue. "As long as the kids are doing lessons, there is not much we can do about the situation." (Oh really? Shouldn't the board have more authority than that?) I felt discouraged and helpless, annoyed and frustrated, unsure in what direction to proceed.

Family Preservation had reason to believe Mom was drinking heavily. She was crafty and able to slip through their fingers. I could not seem to get Elsa on anything, and Katie would not talk.

A week later, Henry and Elsa called me. Mr. and Mrs. Halbrook claimed that Katie was "freaking out." I heard Katie scream in the background. Katie did not know I was on the phone, listening. Katie had always been so sweet and quiet. I couldn't believe this was the same Katie. Did she have a personality disorder? It was not just how loud she was but the rage I detected in her voice. I told the Halbrooks that I would be right over. I arrived in fifteen minutes. By then Katie was quiet and subdued, back to her usual self. I told Katie the truth, that I had heard her screaming over the phone, and I wanted to know what happened. Katie did not say anything; she had shut down and was docile. So I instructed her that she needed to come with me. I proceeded to lead her outside to the white Stratus state car. We both got inside the car.

"Katie, you won't tell me what's going on, so I have to guess here. My guess is that you are angry at your family. You are angry at them because you don't like the way things are done at your home. That is why you are full of rage. You try to hold it in until you can't take it anymore. And I want to tell you that it is okay that you feel that way." At that comment, Katie, who had been staring straight ahead, turned and looked at me. I looked Katie right in the eyes and continued. "You don't have to be like your family. That is okay. You don't want to turn out like them. I don't want you to have to be like them either. Hey, you could be someone special one day."

Katie finally replied. She admitted that she hated her mother's drinking. She hated the way things were at home. Everyone ganged up on her. I asked why, but Katie didn't know. I knew why. Her family didn't like that she wouldn't go along with the program. They wanted Katie to accept and go along with their facade. They did not want a rebelling child who did not like the way they lived.

I was happy that at least we'd identified some of the issues in play. Before I left, I gave Katie my business card. I told her to call if she ever needed my support in times of tension. Katie surprised me by calling me. She began to call me daily: she was simultaneously funny, happy, silly, angry. I always knew what was going on with Katie at that point but was somewhat limited in how much time I could devote to her. She was a confused young girl who wanted someone to listen and vent to, someone who could show empathy toward her and validate her self-worth.

What utterly amazed me was Katie's transformation through this all. Katie started as a somber young girl but evolved into a giggly and self-confident kid during our conversations. Why? I would let her voice be heard, so that her own needs could be met. I felt glad that I could provide Katie with the type of encouragement Katie so desperately needed. I had asked my supervisor early on if I could remove Katie and place her in foster care because she was struggling. He brushed it off and advised me to see about getting her counseling. I thought she could benefit from counseling as well.

Katie once told me she had to sleep in the closet, but I was in a hurry and thought I had misheard her. She was giggling and happy at the time. I let it drop, figuring if I'd heard right, I would know quickly enough because truth does not just vanish. Katie would sometimes call her mom the b-word. I told Katie that is not proper for someone her age to swear and said that when she did so in that horrible tone of voice she sounded just like her mother. I told Katie I did not want her to emulate her mother. I wanted her to be her own sweet self.

Several weeks after that special day with Katie, I received a phone call from an ex-neighbor of Katie's family. Mrs. Reardon called me. She was excited and agitated and wanted me to come over to her house as soon as I could make it. I told Mrs. Reardon that I would try to be there within the hour. Mrs. Reardon seemed happy with that. She gave me their address and said they would be waiting for me. If I had given it any thought, which I wanted to, I would have talked my way out of going there, due to the volume of work bestowed upon us. Life was just moving too fast to even think most of the time. But I dashed right out there instead of giving it thought.

When I arrived, we all sat around and exchanged pleasantries. I was thrilled Katie had a good network of nice friends like these people. They lived in a well-maintained house in an affluent neighborhood. They were a normal, solid family in the community, involved with their church.

Mrs. Reardon told me one of her children was adopted. It might have been Anna.

I spoke alone with Mrs. Reardon first. She told me that Katie was good friends with Anna. Katie had confided something important to Anna. Mrs. Reardon said Katie had been talking about how bad things were at her house. I nodded for her to go on. Mrs. Reardon did not waste time. She exclaimed that Elsa would withhold food from Katie, though Mr. Halbrook, who was an invalid, would sneak Katie food behind Elsa's back. Mrs. Reardon told me Katie had fewer privileges than the other kids. Then time seemed frozen when Mrs. Reardon finally divulged the worst of it all: Elsa made Katie sleep in the little hall closet. I felt suspended in time, dumbfounded. I had heard Mrs. Reardon quite clearly, but I asked her to repeat herself. I couldn't quite fathom that my ears were hearing the information correctly. I felt I was having a revelation. It reminded me of the book *A Child Called It*. The mom singled out one child and half-starved the boy, beat him, and made him sleep in the freezing basement. Though CPS was called a number of times, the mom acted like nothing had happened, and the boy was too petrified to say anything. Because of all the marks on him that the school observed and because he was so thin and so hungry, the school had to step up their involvement.

After reading that book, I realized sadly that the children who seem most robotic or neutral are usually the ones who are most afraid. This makes our job very tricky. We deal with a number of people who could win academy awards for their performances. I feel it is the kids who are frozen in fear we need to hone in on when their fear knows no voice. Not an easy thing to do.

I thought back to when I'd first conducted the investigation. The first time I came out to the Halbrook's house, I asked where Katie slept, and Katie showed me a run-down room with no furniture, a dirty old mattress with no sheet on it laying on the floor. To address the children's needs I decided I would hook the family up with services, and I did, to address the lack of furnishings and the neglected state of the house.

I was having trouble keeping my cool. I was very dedicated to the children I served in my job. I felt it was my *duty* to protect and assist. And yes, I can honestly say that I even loved these kids who had so little or who were treated so poorly. It does not make me the best mother; it does not mean I was the best worker or even that I made the best decisions in my life or with my job performance. But my desire to help and protect the children I am involved with was spot on.

All I could do was to move quickly on the situation and act. I was not in a position to condone but to improve matters, whatever it took, whatever the consequences. So first I asked to speak to Anna. Mrs. Reardon left the room, and Anna entered. Anna was a well-balanced, adorable little twelve- or thirteen-year-old girl; she told me how Katie's family mistreated her, using various examples. What she had to say did not sound rehearsed at all. I used an interview technique where I asked open-ended questions; she responded with detailed answers. "Anna," I said with a smile, encouraging her to not be afraid, as if we were just friends, "where does Katie sleep when she is at home, do you know?" Anna replied without missing a beat that Katie slept in the hall closet. I asked Anna if Katie had told her this or how else did she know? Anna stated in a matter-of-fact manner, "I slept over there once, and they made her sleep in the closet that night too."

I knew that this middle-class, churchgoing family had no ulterior motives. They would not say it unless it were true. My gut told me so. I thanked Anna and asked her to send Katie in the room. Katie came in, shy and nervous, like she had done something wrong, when in fact she was the victim here. I asked how she liked coming over to the Reardons' house to spend time. She replied she liked it a lot. They took her to church with them and did other nice activities with her. I talked with Katie for a little bit longer in general but could not put off the subject any longer. "Katie, I need to know. Where do you sleep when you are at home?" She averted her eyes, and her voice dropped lower. She told me with shame in her voice that she was forced to sleep in the closet. I could not contain my anger very well, so I told Katie, "You won't be doing that much longer, I promise you that!"

I told Katie to stay with the Reardons, and I would get back to them. I raced back to the office and talked with my supervisor. I said I needed to file a dependency petition on Katie. A dependency meant the state of Arizona would take custody of Katie, and I would be her legal guardian. I would try to place her in an appropriate home, like at the Reardons' house, or a group home if needed. My supervisor was wonderful as far as I was concerned (though he was later fired, among others), but apparently we did not see eye to eye.

My supervisor said if the child was sleeping in the closet, that was not necessarily a safety issue. Our job was strictly to keep the children safe. I was not very pleased with his answer. I told him she was not emotionally safe, that the mom withheld food, even if the dad did bring the child food behind her mom's back.

Emotional abuse is a broad field. Emotional abuse is hard to prove in court, and it is hard to get parents to cooperate and go for psychological evaluations, knowing certain statements could be held against them. The psychological evaluations were tools to help determine the parents' mental status and assess if they needed a psychiatric evaluation or meds. Emotional abuse was understood in less definitive terms.

"Did Katie seem afraid?" he asked me.

"No," I snapped, "but she hates having to sleep in a closet and has every right as a human being to not be forced to do so. That is mental cruelty." I was remembering *A Child Called It* and how long the system had to fail that child until the authorities could finally step in and save him. My supervisor and I went a few rounds. Finally we decided on a plan. I would have Katie brought to the office to talk with Dr. Sheeley, our onsite psychologist. Dr. Sheeley would do an assessment, and we would take it from there. I scheduled the appointment in the book; reserving the time and date in Dr. Sheeley's appointment book was protocol and all we had to do. Generally she was available all day Tuesday, so I had to schedule it for a few weeks from then. I patiently awaited the appointment.

I remembered back to the last time I had been to Elsa and Henry's. I had asked to speak to Katie when I went over to the Halbrooks' house. Elsa had called Katie in such a nasty tone of voice that I had snapped at her. "Don't talk to her in that tone of voice. She didn't do anything wrong!" Elsa looked shocked; she had never seen me show my other side. But it was there, that other side. As I mentioned previously, usually I try hard to be congenial and friendly. As a matter of fact, on that visit, I had sat around with the family for a while, and I kept telling Katie how beautiful she was.

And indeed Katie was. She was of medium height, medium built, with sandy-blonde layered hair and pretty blue green eyes, a small nose and freckles. I kept repeating how pretty she was because Katie confided to me on the phone that her mother kept calling her ugly. To further rub it in on my end, I said to her parents and sibling, "I don't know why Katie would say she isn't pretty. You guys really need to tell her that she is pretty more." Elsa probably wanted to throw daggers at me when I was leaving, but I was only doing my job, as far as I was concerned. I know if I had confronted Elsa with the comment about calling Katie ugly, she would have just denied it.

The day of the appointment with Dr. Sheeley came and went. I was the one who wound up bringing Katie to the appointment, as Mrs. Reardon was unable to do so that day, and Katie's parents did not have a car. I did not keep the appointment from them; I said, "We need to assess Katie since you guys have so much conflict. Perhaps she needs psychological counseling." They agreed to it. If Elsa hadn't agreed to it, she would have had a big argument with me, and I think she wanted to avoid getting into matches over Katie. When I received the assessment back from Dr. Sheeley, I was excited. It was stated right in her report that Katie had told Dr. Sheeley Katie slept in the closet and didn't like it. I was energized, and I went over to the Halbrooks' house to finally confront them with the news in the report: my ammunition.

I started reading the report to the Halbrooks after exchanging hellos and a few pleasantries. I did not go there to show them how nasty I could be but to show them how nasty their treatment of their daughter was, at least as far as I was concerned. When I got to the part about Katie sleeping in the closet, Elsa replied in a matter-of-fact manner, "Oh, Katie chooses to do that—we don't make her do it." My response to Elsa's comment was, "Well, I have a problem with that if she chooses to sleep in the closet and you let her, and I have a problem with that if she doesn't choose to sleep in the closet and you make her." I told them I did not feel Katie was safe or stable staying there and said I would see if the Reardons would allow her to stay at their house.

Though I should have filed a dependency on Katie, I settled for doing a safety monitor plan, since my supervisor would not let me file a dependency. However, I did need Elsa and Henry to sign the paper first. I don't think either of them wanted to, for entirely different reasons. Elsa had picked Katie as her scapegoat and wanted to continue with her agenda. Henry, with tears in his eyes, did not feel Katie was safe and, unlike Elsa, he loved Katie very much. Yet, while he vouched the love he felt for his daughter, he did not want to relinquish her to someone else. I explained to Henry that he could not protect her, so she needed to go.

I went over to the Reardons' house, where Mrs. Reardon also signed the paper. I explained that with a safety monitor plan, the safety monitor has to be in the presence of the parent with the child 24-7. The child could not be left alone with the parent. That is what the paperwork stated and what the individuals were signing their names to. If a person violated the safety plan, a dependency would then be filed, and the safety monitor could no longer be a foster placement. (If we can't trust a monitor the first time, most likely we can't trust that person the next time, or the time after that either.)

The next time I saw Katie, she was finally enrolled in public school and like a new person: happy, more outgoing, more relaxed. The safety monitor plan took Katie away from the emotional abuse at home without court involvement. Family Preservation then had the Reardons and Halbrooks do a power of attorney for legal reasons basic to the situation. In the meantime, Cindy, Katie's sixteen-year-old sister, had a baby, and the baby tested positive for marijuana. Because of the fact that Cindy was still a minor, and adding in Elsa and Henry's many other prior CPS reports, the baby was taken into CPS custody. Later, Katie was no longer staying with the Reardons, Katie and her sisters were all taken into custody.

I was unaware of what happened; I was able to close out my case with the family, and I was covering a different zip code at that time. Apparently there had been another fight between Mom and Katie. Ryan, the new worker, decided enough was enough. I can't say I blamed him a bit. Henry and Elsa kept calling me when Ryan had the case, but I told them it was no longer my case. I saw Katie once at the office when she came to visit her parents, and we had a nice conversation. Henry, who'd had exceptionally bad health for a long time, passed away shortly after the girls were taken into custody. Though it was no longer my case, the day after the funeral, I stopped by the house to pay my condolences because I was in the neighborhood. The adult sibling, who didn't live there but was there because of the funeral, was surprised to see me but said he would pass my message on to Elsa.

What must she have been feeling? First she lost her kids to CPS, then her husband. While I never approved of Elsa's ways, especially her treatment of Katie, I still felt bad for her loss of Henry.

Everyone constantly comments on how mean CPS workers are. The truth of the matter is that most of us are not mean. We are like any other human beings walking the face of the earth—maybe a little more hard core, due to the nature of our work. We do, as a whole, care about the kids we are involved with; we are concerned about children's safety. We do see some incredibly ugly situations that shock us to the point where after a while it is no longer a shock. We become less sensitized as a sanity or survival mechanism; in addition to the large volume of work we do, we are generally too exhausted to overreact. We have to be constantly thinking of liability, politics, and the media coming after us if anything goes wrong.

I am guessing that policemen go through a similar scenario. But police can carry guns and have a lot more authority than CPS workers do in a certain realm. They also experience different kinds of risks than we do. I watch those investigation shows and feel so much compassion for officers who cry over dead victims. They are elated when they can bring families of the victims justice to some degree. Kudos to law enforcement everywhere! You are underappreciated and deserve better recognition!

I know it haunts me every time I hear a little kid who comes to our CPS office to visit his or her parents crying after the visit is over. I feel at that second so unhappy with the job I do, like I am cursed. We CPS workers experience burnout easily because of both the amount of work and pressures of the job. We have tons and tons of paperwork. There was a time, for example, when they changed the child-safety assessment. It grew from approximately ten to twenty pages of work to eighty pages per case. An investigator is assigned four-plus cases per week. That is almost like writing a small book a week! Or at least it felt that way. Of course, if you weren't the kind of worker who did your job the way you were supposed to or who didn't care, it didn't matter. Good luck to the rest of us poor suckers!

As far as conducting the investigations: we might go to people's homes and miss them and have to come back a few times until each member of the family is seen. By policy, we are generally required to interview the children at their schools. Can you imagine? Sometimes there are six or seven kids in a family, and we might have to go to two or three schools, plus the home or homes of the parents. We must also attend tons of meetings. We sometimes have to go to training classes. When there is a removal, it seems like more times than not we have to transport the child all the way to the other side of town to place the child in a foster placement. If the removal involves a number of kids scattered in different placements, it could take hours to find the placements and drop them off.

"Oh, we know all about you CPS workers" is a common line we hear. Luckily I have heard this kind of comment a lot less than some. I love the kids and what they symbolize to me: innocence, hopefulness, a promise of a new tomorrow. Sometimes their innocence is shadowed and clouded over by others' pasts. I stand and fight for children to have the right to be innocent and to be able to play, be carefree, have fun, maintaining hope, knowing this has brought me a sense of greater meaning and deeper faith while performing my job. My reward: kids of all ages smiling at me, some thanking me with a look or a picture, seeing a glimmer of hope in their eyes. Later, when I switched to working in ongoing units, I would watch children suffering from neglect and emotional problems blossom and become, to an extent, healed and happy, or at least capable of having happy moments instead of existing within a world comprised of blank stares. Knowing that kids sometimes are able to have a better life because I entered their life for a brief moment and could help advocate for them affects me.

5

Ed's Sex Abuse Case

Ed's sex abuse case involved a little eleven-year-old Mexican girl. Ed needed backup on the case and called our office for it. I agreed to go out and assist him. When I got to the run-down apartments, Ed was interviewing the dad. Ed told the parents the child had to leave and go stay with relatives. He was offering no other choice. Since the parents only spoke Spanish, Ed told me in English that the parents had used the child like a servant. For one thing, she was not permitted to go to school. She had to stay home and clean, as well as take care of her toddler siblings. To add insult to injury, Dad decided to sexually abuse the child. Ed and I were both fuming, although our tone of voice belied the fact. We had to stay neutral while Ed was conducting his investigation.

Ed asked me to take the little girl outside so he could drill the parents a little more while we waited for relatives to show up. The relatives were to be the safety monitors, so the child could be placed with family, instead of having to go to a foster home. As the little girl and I walked outside, she started to cry. I badly wanted to hug her and tell her everything would be all right. But would it? I did not know that answer.

I gently rested my hand on her shoulder and said, "Listen real carefully to me, please. Look into my eyes." She did as told. I proceeded to say slowly and clearly, "I know you are so sad and hurt today, but please remember one thing, if you remember nothing else about this day. Remember that your parents are from a different culture and country, and they might do things differently there. But *you* are in America, and you have the right to be treated a certain way. We won't let you be treated the way you have been treated here by your parents, in this country. Do you hear me? Do you understand?" I asked her. And through her puddle of tears and quivering lip this little girl nodded yes, she did understand. And she knew I cared. Or so I thought. I was afraid I was going to cry while I was speaking to her. I felt like it was a special one-time oath I needed to take to continue to do my job and that she was the person who would tell me if I'd passed or failed. God, what an emotional moment we shared!

I told her to remember one other thing. "Remember that what happened today and everything leading up to today was not your fault. If anybody tries to blame you, know this was not your fault." I kind of tilted my head and smiled a little with narrowed eyes; I was facing the sun and felt it was important to not talk with my sunglasses on, which would have shielded the truth pouring from my eyes into hers.

The little girl had stopped crying by then. She nodded and looked wise, sad, and determined to go on, to thrive, to be a normal eleven-year-old child, though one would swear at that second she was chronologically more like twenty-two years old instead of merely eleven. I then emphasized who I was and said it was my job to protect her. I asked if she was okay. She said she was.

We waited in a solemn kind of silence until her relatives came to pick her up to go live with them. If I'd read their looks correctly when they got to the apartment complex, I saw they had no intention of blaming anything on this little girl, and I breathed a sigh of relief as I drove back to my office. May God protect the innocent and allow them to thrive and grow.

6

Maria Contore

There was a mom who had a few kids. The oldest was a boy, Juan. Juan was on probation for possession of marijuana. Maria had married, and there was friction between the stepdad and Juan. One day it escalated, so Mom called Juan's probation officer. the juvenile probation officer (JPO) wound up putting Juan in juvenile detention. Mom did not bother to show up for his release. She was working. The jail contacted CPS, and I went to pick Juan up upon his release. I was mad when I took Juan home. I wanted to talk to this "wonderful" mother, who couldn't care less.

I was greeted by the aunt when we arrived at Juan's house. I told the aunt that Juan seemed like a nice enough boy and asked what was up with Mom. The aunt admitted the conflict was between Juan and the stepdad. Also, Juan was finally doing well in school, but the stepdad had a job transfer to Las Vegas, and the family was going to move. Juan had been lingering around, and he said that if he didn't finish his probation before moving, he would be in trouble. The aunt was not going to be moving with the family, so I asked how she felt about Juan finishing the semester (he would be done with probation by then) or if she would consider allowing him finish high school while living with her in Arizona. She was more than willing to do so. She got along fine with Juan.

I talked with Mom, and she also agreed to the plan. I told her that Juan felt the stepdad was a threat to him, and he missed the relationship with his own biological father. I said he also might be feeling insecure about Mom's new closeness with her husband; Juan might feel as if he were playing second fiddle to this new dad. Mom brushed it off as unimportant. But when I mentioned it to Juan, he agreed that that was the truth. I put in for counseling services to attempt to help Juan cope with those feelings. I was relieved to see that Mom went along with everything and demonstrated in her own way that she would miss Juan, that she did want him to join them after they moved, despite her ignorance of his feelings.

When I stopped at the house and asked Mom how she and Juan were getting along, I found out Juan and Maria had not spoken to each other since he was in detention. I asked her to call Juan into the room. Mom proceeded to ask the sister to call Juan to come into the living room where we were talking. Juan came into the room. They were standing side by side, mother and son. I put my fingers up around my eyes, pretending my fingers were glasses. I looked back and forth from Mom to Juan and back to Mom.

Finally I walked over to them, put one hand on Mom's shoulder and one hand on Juan's shoulder, and made them turn inward, so they were finally facing each other. I said, "Okay now, please hug and kiss each other and tell each other 'I love you.'" They hugged and kissed, and Mom said, "I love you." Juan didn't say anything back. "You do love your mother, don't you Juan?" I chided him. "Yeah," he replied, "but I don't want to have to say it." All three of us cracked up laughing, and on that note I left, happy.

With CPS, some days are better than others. As a worker, I feel lucky when I have a good day because most of them are not good at all.

7

Case of the Mouse

I took someone who was in training with me on an investigation to a young mom's house. The house was in a semi-run-down neighborhood. From the outside, the house did not look bad. The child, a little female toddler, looked healthy and was sweet, with curly dark hair and dark eyes. She was about four years old and was dancing around. She was a pint-size version of her pretty but very young mom.

The house was a little dirty, but manageable. The report was about the filthy living conditions. Pat and I were all ready to leave when, lo and behold, I saw a little creature scamper across the floor. "What was that? What was that?" I repeated that phrase over and over, frantically. I knew darn well it was a mouse, and in order to prevent myself from screaming at the idea of a mouse, I had to say something instead, to steady my nerves. But I couldn't stop saying, "What was that?"

Then I added, "You don't want that thing getting its germs all over your beautiful little girl, do you?" With that, the pretty mom broke down into tears. I could tell I had made her feel quite ashamed and inferior. I turned to her spontaneously and hugged her. My purpose was not to put her to shame but to try to impress on her a sense of motivation. She was too young and very beautiful; perhaps she had too much responsibility, more than she needed.

I looked her straight in the eye and commented, "Listen, I didn't want to make you feel bad. I don't think that is the solution to the problem. I'm sorry I have done that. I want you to do better, not to feel bad. Tell you what. When I leave, get some traps or some powder to kill or scare off the rodents." I inspected her house and found a hole where the rodents could come in. I also suggested that if she had a relative or male friend to ask that person very nicely if maybe he could patch up the hole for her. I smiled hopefully; she giggled and nodded yes.

A week later, I went back to reinspect her home. It looked better. The hole was barricaded. The trash was empty. There were no dirty dishes in the sink. Somehow I felt if we were a team, and we had accomplished our goal: to make things better by thinking or planning and then executing the best plan. This was primarily achieved not by berating a struggling young mom but through trying to motivate her with encouragement and a sense of pride to do the right thing, starting with keeping a clean and orderly house for sanitary reasons and for her child's well-being.

I'm happy to say no more reports were called on this family, and the young mom, realizing that she needed a support system and assistance to help guide her along, did accept services.

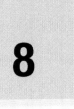

8

Lena Moreno

The dependency for Lena Moreno was a private petition filed by the Guardian ad Litem GAL on behalf of the maternal grandmother. The grandmother wanted legal custody of the children, since Lena had left the two kids at Grandma's house for a long, long time. When I went to see the children, Carina and Alberto, they had different things to say about their mom. Alberto was a little softer on his mom. He missed her and minimized Mom's lack of parenting skills. The grandma said that Alberto had Mom's disposition and the same possible bipolar issues as well. *Great,* I thought, *just what he doesn't need, poor kid.*

The sister seemed to know the score a little better than her brother. She did not favor her mother. She complimented Grandma for being there for them. Carina remembered that when she was little, her mom was driving with the kids and was arrested. Carina did not remember the particulars, or perhaps she just did not understand them at her tender age then. In any case, the police hauled their mom off to jail, and Grandma came to again take the kids.

At the beginning of the case, it was next to impossible to track Lena down. Grandma explained that Lena had gotten married about five years earlier. The husband had been a fairly good influence on her. Lena stopped using methamphetamines at the time. Lena even got a job and held it down for a year or two. However, even during that time the kids lived with their grandma. I wasn't impressed by such a consistent lack of attachment, to put it mildly. Grandma also told me that after the five years, Mom was once again unemployed and using drugs again. At one point Lena and her husband had come to live at Grandma's house, but Mom got high and out of control in front of the children. I asked how the grandma could tell. "Oh, you could tell all right," Grandma replied. "It was easy to tell. Lena started getting all hyped up, and her temper started giving way. She became restless, irrational, and was disregarding house rules, as well as boundaries." This was just one of many versions of moms using meth and losing their kids.

When I finally tracked Lena down, she was staying in a tiny, sleazy, one-bedroom apartment in a bad neighborhood. Boxes were piled up all over the place. Lena was a tall, big girl. She almost resembled Alice in Wonderland when Alice took the pill that made her too big for the house. Lena recounted a similar story to what Grandma had relayed about Mom: using and then getting off drugs for a number of years, then going back on the drugs. I asked why she went back to them and received one of those "because" (because nothing!) type of answers. Currently, Lena was trying to get off the drugs again. She was at least perceptive enough to be aware of her kids' anger issues over deserting them.

Could anyone blame them? Yoyo Lena, when does it all end? Lena said she wanted "to make it up to them." I wondered if they believed that line, because I did not. In the end, Lena did seem to get her act together. Well, saying "in the end" is relative to the time frame in which I worked the case. By then I had worked with the family for several months before passing the case on to the ongoing unit. At that time, Lena and her husband had moved from the horrible dump they lived in into a really nice house. It was owned by someone Lena had known, a godmother who was rooting for Lena to clean up her act.

Lena was also getting help for her bipolar disorder and taking her meds. Lena and her mom had made up. I was glad about that, because it definitely affected the kids. Speaking of the kids, they were going for weekend visits to Lena's house. Lena had a parent aide who brought the kids to Mom. After a while, Lena had unsupervised visits.

Lena wanted her kids back. I am not sure of the outcome, if she got them back fully or partially. I don't know if the dependency was dismissed or not. I am not sure if she deserved them back, but that might have been my own stern judgment upon her. It's too bad Lena had to lose ten years' worth of her life without her kids being there—for what? Harsh drugs that ruin a person's life and set a bad example for the children. Anyway, at least Lena had made an attempt to change. Better late than not at all.

The main thing perhaps was that the kids did seem happy to have Lena back and trying. The last I heard or saw of the case involved some paperwork. Lena still was dropping urinalysis (UAs). Instead of sending the results of the UAs to the correct ongoing worker, the TASC people (Tasc is the name of the organization CPS uses for parents in a local drug testing program) sent it to me, the investigator. I noticed before I interofficed the paperwork over to ongoing that Mom had once again slipped on her UAs. The pattern was pretty repetitious. Old habits die hard.

Good lesson for Lena's kids and all kids: watch what habits you pick up in your life. They might come back to haunt you, even when you think you've put them to rest. Best to also remember that some habits are worse than others and do not die easy.

Due to the age of her children, there was no severance in Lena's case. Even if Mom could not reunify with her kids, most likely Grandma would be their guardian, or they would just age out in the Young Adult Program (YAP) instead of severing the parent's rights regarding the children.

9

Mindy, Yvette, and Tomas

There was a cute six year-old female child named Mindy. The mom had called in a report pertaining to the dad, claiming the stepmom and stepsisters were scaring Mindy when she went there on weekend visits. I can't recall how scared Mindy was of them, but upon delving further, I discovered that the child was afraid of Mom. Mom hit her with a belt. Mindy was too afraid to tell me, but her older brother disclosed this when I went to see him and Mindy at their elementary school. It did not take long to figure out that Mom was trying to force the child to turn against her dad. The child felt conflicted because she did not want to turn against him.

When I went to talk to Tomas, the father, I saw he was a soft-spoken person who cared very much about his child. He brought out a tape recorder and played a tape recording of Mom screaming loud and abusively at their child. Though I know limited Spanish and had to bring an interpreter with me on the case, I could tell just by Mom's tone of voice that she was abusive. Dad and the stepmom further described the mom as being very manipulative. The other thing was that Mom didn't want the child to come over to Dad's because the child would have fun when she did go for the weekend. The pressure was so great that when Mindy went to stay over, she started to wet the bed. The dad and stepmom reassured Mindy not to worry about that or anything else when she was at their house.

During this time, Mindy got into trouble at school once. Mindy fought with a kid and tried telling the teacher the other kid had started the fight. When both parents, both students, and the teacher had a conference, Mindy recanted her story immediately. The stepmom was leery of this behavior, and I was as well. I was fearful the child was already picking up Mom's undesirable tendencies: lying, manipulation, anger. I had great concerns and scheduled Mindy for an appointment with our onsite psychologist, Dr. Sheeley. Dr. Sheeley confirmed my suspicions: the child loved both parents but was being put in the middle to choose sides, which was not healthy. I went over the psychology report with both parents. Hopefully they cared enough and got the message. Maybe. There were no more CPS reports after that one on their family.

10

Warren Howard

Warren Howard was a seventeen-year-old kid whose mom deserted him when she was evicted from her apartment. Mom was a hard-core meth addict who had turned her son onto methamphetamines at the very young age of nine. Warren wanted help. At the point when I met him he was homeless, hearing voices and having hallucinations. He was basically a very nice boy. He was tall, lanky, quiet, with short hair, dark features, and very good manners. I was angry about his poor excuse for a mother.

Warren blamed his dad too. I'm not sure if that was totally fair or not. Warren's dad, Jose, had been in Iraq off and on for the last five years, more on than off, and had just returned home. Jose had no idea what his ex had been doing to the boy. As a matter of fact, Warren said that they had been a happy family until Mom one day decided to leave dad. Warren said that everything fell apart after that.

Warren was sent to a group home, Just for Boys, which he ran away from, then returned to, then ran away from again. The last time Warren returned, we decided to send him to Canyon State Academy. Boys who went AWOL a lot or had behavioral problems in general were sent there. The place was run like a military school. The kids attended classes, spent part of the time as if they were in a basic training course, and were given responsibilities, such as doing chores.

It was the shock of my life when Warren's hallucinations ended after he started taking meds. The psychologist told me that it was part of Warren's bipolar condition and was treatable, obviously true based on the astounding results. Warren felt bad he didn't get to see his dad enough. However, after a period of time, the child did spend weekends at his dad's house. Warren was then transferred to a regular group home much closer to where his dad lived.

One weekend, his dad's fiancée, a nice girl named Darcy who genuinely liked Warren, found out she was pregnant and felt quite ill. She also had two little boys of her own. So feeling the way she did, she wanted to rest. Jose had asked Warren to skip that particular weekend instead of coming to spend it with them. Warren became despondent apparently, because he then ran away. Dad and Darcy were totally surprised and dismayed at the turn of events.

Nobody knows where Warren disappeared to. I contacted a local state agency, OSI, office of Special Investigations), which specializes in conducting investigations with CPS in some cases. I gave them information in the hope that they could track Warren down, but without any luck. I also put in a motion for law enforcement to pick him up, which didn't help. It is assumed by myself and others that Warren went back to his old life after being clean for six months. Old habits die hard. I would like to add that young people with those kind of "old" habits die young.

The only consolation I received concerning Warren was when I discovered his mother was the one who had gotten him on meth: I called her then-working cell phone and left a message, trying to make Mom feel like the scum she was. "Fine if you want to throw your life down the tubes, but how can you do that to your own son?" I asked her. I even tried calling back, but the number was disconnected by then.

I imagined her getting high, crying, "But I do love my son," and continuing her filthy habits, lies, and lame rationalizations while doing drugs. I also wondered if Mom loved Warren enough to destroy his life entirely or just enough to help him along the way on his path of destruction.

11

Kylee Brady

I received a report about Kylee and her two kids, who were living in horrendous conditions. They had been evicted from their house but were still there. I went out to conduct the investigation and found that the boyfriend and father of the baby, Lorio, had called the report in. Kylee told me she had dumped him for battering her and that he'd called the report in as revenge. I believed her. I talked to him and made a plan to meet with him, but he never showed up. I thought, *Yep, just as I suspected. He does have something to hide, or why isn't he here?* I waited at his mother's house for about an hour before I gave up on him and left.

I provided Kylee with services. She wasn't a bad mom, just broken and feeling a bit defeated. She had chosen two loser men in her life who helped her to get nowhere good. Kylee told me that her mom had a lot of money, but the two of them were estranged. Kylee would rather suffer than go begging to her mom. I understood that she had pride. Maybe that was a redeeming quality in her, or maybe it was a hindrance. Maybe Kylee's mom expected the impossible from Kylee, and Kylee couldn't stand the pressure.

Our good Family Builders team stayed with Kylee and helped her out quite a bit. They provided food baskets, counseling, and so on. I was happy for Kylee when Family Builders advised me they'd found her a decent job and reported that she was doing much better. She was also staying at a friend's, who put her up in a nice apartment complex. I looked at the sky and said, "Thank you, God" because I was so glad to hear that nice news.

12

Carmen Lenore

_____

Carmen was a rather beautiful twenty something female, petite, reasonably bright and personable, with long brown hair. She had one child, Gregory, age six, whom the report was about. I remember that Gregory was in diapers and could only roll on the floor. I was not sure of his diagnosis, nor perhaps did I ask. I cannot remember at this point. He could not speak. He was the size of a nine-month old. Gregory had a tube for feeding purposes. He was adorable. As I talked to Carmen, I was 100 percent focused on Gregory. He and I were smiling at each other. My sole purpose for being at the house was to discuss Gregory's safety when he was strapped in his wheelchair, before he was put on the school bus. The source of the report, the bus driver, claimed that Gregory was not secured into his wheelchair.

That was pretty much the whole investigation at that particular time. The source had also claimed that Carmen was high as a kite a few times when she came to pick Gregory up and that he wasn't strapped in well in the morning, either, unless Gregory Sr. had strapped him in. Gregory Sr. had no problem strapping Gregory in his wheelchair. I decided that from then Gregory Sr. would be responsible for attending to Gregory Jr. before and after school. That would have been the end of the story except that I had contracted one of our service providers, Family Builders, to check on the family. In the course of their doing so several months later, I received a downright gruesome email.

The email stated that Carmen had deserted her family. She was hanging out with a bad crowd. Carmen and her drug-user friends had kidnapped a man and held him prisoner, which made the local news. What they did to this poor man was almost unspeakable; they tortured him into writing checks for them to cash.

I was utterly amazed that they released Carmen from jail so rapidly. They'd either allowed her to bail out or just released her. Though I told myself not to be biased against Carmen, I was. I thought, *What a lowlife*, committing that kind of crime just so she and her lowlife friends could do more meth and destroy more brain cells, especially when she had such a loving and decent family at home. Gregory was the father of only two of her children, but he took charge. In good faith, I could not stomach returning the kids to their mom if they had split. It was stated in our safety assessment that anyone who committed a crime centered around the use of drugs endangered their kids' safety. Wasn't that what she, in fact, did?

Carmen told me she did not know they had taken the guy prisoner and that she was not present when the rest of the gang tortured him. I wasn't feeling overly kindly toward lovely Carmen. Carmen was dumbfounded when I said that the kids would have to stay with Gregory if they broke up, and I recommended he seek a custody order. If they didn't break up, our department would be watching her. Did she think I would tell her, "Sure, go take them. You're done with dope and crime now; no sweat. Do what you want."

Carmen, that guy lost his limb, and probably in the long run you lost your kids, I would venture to guess. You were lucky to have Gregory Sr. protect your kids as long as possible ... and love and care for them.

It was no surprise Carmen never dropped a UA as required. She probably also refused the services we put in for her as well.

13

The Case of Jana Ortiz and Getting Cases Transferred To Ongoing

After Carmen's case, I had a dependency case. The boy was about eleven, and his name was Nick. He had gotten into a little trouble and was supposed to go to a juvenile hearing. His mom did not show up in time. Therefore, the guardian ad litem filed a private petition for CPS to take custody of Nick.

The mom, Jana, loved Nick a lot. The problem with Jana was that she was still doing meth and probably loved her meth a little more than Nick. Or maybe doing meth was just easier for Jana than putting in the effort to be a real mom. Jana had been homeless on and off for some time since her husband went to prison. Her priorities were horrible, inexcusable. Nicholas Sr. had been in prison for at least several years due to crimes committed to sustain his drug habit.

Nick had missed a lot of school over the last few years, with Mom moving and being homeless. Nick was on probation for pulling some dumb little stunt at his school. He had filled the radiator of the school car with dishwashing detergent or some lotion. He was probably doing it for the attention he did not get at home.

Nick had an adult sibling, Lola, a lovely girl of about twenty, who had two little boys, ages two and three. Lola also had a nice boyfriend, Stephano, the father of the kids. I remember that Stephano and Lola were always polite and very mature for being such young adults. They probably were put in positions where they'd had to grow up too fast. The short of it was that we placed Nick with his sister. At that time, our Glendale office was having trouble getting cases transferred to the ongoing unit.

I had prepared my case to be transferred within thirty days, but it took six months before that happened. I sometimes think it was accidentally because of my email that cases got transferred at all when they did.

I had emailed our big boss at the Glendale office, asking when the cases would be transferred. He showed me emails he had sent, trying to get these cases transferred out, to no avail. Then had a brainstorm, or so I thought at the time. I decided to email the head of our district, a person by the name of Sally, about our dilemma. I sent an email that roughly said, "Ya know, Sal, everyone is aware that Glendale has one of the worst turnover rates of all the offices. The fact that we can't get these cases transferred out after six months doesn't help matters at all."

What I didn't know when I sent the email was that Sally had transferred from our region (West) to the East Valley, so the issue no longer concerned her. Therefore, when she received the email, she automatically forwarded it to one of the top administrators. All I know was that the big boss of our facility, the assistant program manager (APM) chewed me out for "breaking protocol." He told me that I was a great worker but that I'd "better watch the emails." I think he gave me too much credit. I wasn't a great worker, more like average, but I did try to be diligent. Anyway, I shrugged my shoulders; does a leopard change spots? I wasn't even sure what the big deal was, but my guess is that working for CPS makes a person overly paranoid and defensive. The agency is very inconsistent about standing behind their employees. (Therefore, his threat was understandable. Sal was actually fired a few years later, a scapegoat.)

My boss kind of lightened up when I showed him that in my

email I'd said it was not his fault that our cases didn't get transferred, that he'd tried to get the files transferred for us, with no luck.

The day after my email went out, all the many cases waiting to be transferred for six months suddenly and mysteriously were taken off our hands. Yippee, what a relief. Both my boss and I were delighted!

Anyway, Jana had originally been AWOL for a long time but resurfaced right before her court date, wanting to do services. Once I transferred from investigations to ongoing, I saw that most of the insincere parents I dealt with used this as their ploy or game tactic. They would disappear until the last minute and then come forward at court wearing their most innocent expression as they said to the judge, "I have been waiting on the case manager to do my services." The only ones they really fooled were themselves. Those determined to get their kids back would do their services and contact their worker and stay proactive, no matter what. And it's hard to reach someone without a current number or address.

The drug program that Jana was engaged in, or that she was supposed to be engaged in, either reported that she was dropping dirty UAs or that she was not dropping any UAs (we considered failing to drop scheduled UAs as the same as dropping dirty UAs). When Jana and I met up, she was staying in a halfway house in Mesa. I felt for her. At least she was trying, or so I thought.

I could be very naïve, despite my age. I learned with time and experience that meth users can be big talkers, and they go through the motions without accomplishing anything at all. When it came to action, there was little to be found with meth users. All hype is the name of that tune.

In between these events, Nicholas had been released from prison and also was staying at a nearby halfway house in Mesa. He was working, so I was more hopeful at the time about Dad than Mom. Lola was getting pressure from her mom, since Mom apparently resented Lola because we'd placed Nick with his sister rather than Jana having custody of him.

When the case was transferred, I was still responsible for doing the report and review (R & R), a special court report, done every three to six months, that updates the court as to the progress of the child or children and the parents. After three R & R's, with one also being a permanency hearing as well as an R &R, a severance trial would be scheduled if the kids were not able to be reunified with the parents.

Since then, I have become much more used to doing R & R reports, as well as the lengthy social history reports in adoptions, but at the time I stumbled through the R & R with much fear and intimidation, since I had never done one. The reason I had to do the R & R was because the cases weren't transferred. Court was even more of a nightmare than doing the court report. The judge asked about services. I was so embarrassed because, while I'd initially hooked Mom up with a bunch of services, once she went AWOL and then resurfaced, I had not resumed her services. I didn't have time to do so because I was busy doing so many investigations and was not used to how ongoing units operated. Additionally, Jana had not seen her son in a month. To the judge, that was a big no-no. In any case, the entire situation left me totally frustrated; I felt like I did let everyone down.

It took me forever to get Lola extra money for Nick's allowances, though I am happy to say it was easy to arrange him a free and rather adorable new bed through a charity group, My Hand Extended. I think the delay of payment for his clothing allowance was because I either had the wrong address listed, because they'd moved several times, or I forgot to enter something in our computer system to activate the payment. I am not the most literate computer user on the planet.

What upset me about Jana was that she got Lola's family evicted because she kept coming around trying to see them at their apartment complex. The landlord knew Jana's reputation for doing drugs, so he held it against poor Lola. Lola was also breaking up with her boyfriend, which I was sad to find out. I wonder if Nick ever went back to his mom, or what the outcome was with Nick and his family. It was still at pretty much the beginning of the case, or barely the middle, so there was still hope to be had. And with Dad out of prison and trying to do things right on his end, maybe he would be a good influence on Mom if she could follow through. Maybe the ongoing worker could help Mom do so. (Somehow, I don't really believe that was the outcome though.)

14

A Spooky Halloween and Safety Not to Be Found in CPS Parking Lots

CPS is not the kind of business where staff dresses up for Halloween. There is enough ghoulishness in our jobs; I am quite sure none of us have the desire to dress up, even if we had been offered the choice. I will never quite forget two days before Halloween in 2006 at our Glendale office. Mind you, the Glendale office was not in the safest of neighborhoods. We covered the Maryvale area and were located between Glendale and Maryvale. Maryvale was a bad area in Phoenix. Women having substance-exposed newborns (SEN) affected by killer methamphetamine was alarmingly commonplace in Maryvale. We saw high school dropouts, felons with a number of kids and no jobs, and immigrants without citizenship on a regular basis.

That particular night, I was ready to leave work. It was quite late by then, around eleven, possibly closer to midnight. I was leaving with another coworker, my buddy, Deb. We walked out the back door to the parking lot where the employees all parked. Though there was a gate, it was barely medium height, and anybody could jump it easily enough. Deb and I were walking when we saw a guy with a long hedge trimmer. He was trimming bushes. All I could think was, *Didn't they just release another* Texas Chainsaw Massacre *movie? Who is this nut working in the dark? Surely they don't have state gardeners trim bushes at midnight?*

Deb read my mind and said, "I'll wait until you get to your car." She was parked up front, and I was parked toward the back. "You mean if I get to my car," was my reply. I started to speed walk. The guy was getting close to where my car was. I quickly jumped inside my car as the hedge trimmer was reaching it; I locked the car doors quickly, backed up, and drove off without a moment's delay. After that night, I always made sure my car was parked up close if I was staying late. And I also decided that if I ever was to see anyone out there again, I'd call the cops instead of making a mad dash for it.

Eventually I transferred to the Thunderbird office in North Phoenix, a much safer area for the most part. But it was still dark and desolate if a worker left late at night, no matter which office we worked at, and parking in a state parking lot did not add extra reassurance for one's safety.

I wound up working at the downtown Mesa office before I quit my job. There are a number of halfway houses in the near vicinity. One night a guy with a crazed look in his eye asked me for money. I did give him spare change. I felt fortunate he didn't try to assault me on the way to my car.

15

Tracy Lindamor

Tracy had a daughter named Justina, about nine or ten. She was lively and inquisitive by nature. The CPS report stated that Tracy left the girl alone all the time. If I recall correctly, the source was the apartment manager. I assured him I would have a talk with Tracy. I went over to their apartment and discovered a gentle, sweet, hard-working black woman with her cute, smiling daughter. Tracy looked very tired and explained that she had to catch several buses both to and from work. This transportation arrangement added an two extra hours to her day, at a minimum.

The girl was nice, but her mom told me the child was a fire starter. She had started a fire in the backyard while Mom was at work. The child's punishment was to attend a class provided by the fire department. When I was interviewing the child, I said in my fake stern voice, "Do you think you'll be starting anymore fires anytime soon?" She shrugged, smiled, and replied, "I hope I have learned my lesson." For some reason, this sounded too rehearsed and not quite promising.

Instead of relying on fate, I came up with one better. I said to Tracy, "How about if we enroll Justina in the Y program for the remainder of the summer? We can have her go after school during the school year. That way she won't have time to start any fires." Tracy looked relieved, as if I had just made her queen for a day, like on the old show. "Here, Tracy, we have your new washer and dryer behind this curtain!" I might as well have pulled out a crown and robe, put them on Tracy, and given her a dozen roses. She sighed with delight and relief. Guess what? So did Justina. It made me realize Justina had started fires out of boredom, seeking attention. Of that I was sure.

16

Lorena Torres

The report we received on Lorena was that she did not pick up her son when the school called asking her to do so. Lorena's boyfriend, Manuel, would usually pick up the child, though he was not the child's father. This particular day, Lorena's boyfriend was apparently running late at work and could not get there in time. The boy, Jesus, five years of age, had special needs. This seemed to stress Lorena.

Manuel was kind and easy to deal with, but Lorena had mental health issues, or at least that was the way she presented. When he found out I was with CPS, he started crying. She yelled at Manuel for being emotional. Lorena, on the other hand, seemed apathetic and belligerent. I told them not to worry, to just make sure the child was picked up the next time.

One day Manuel called me. The couple was having a nasty argument, though it was probably more Lorena's fault, since she always picked fights. Anyway, Manuel said things were real bad and asked if I could I come over and assist. I went as fast I could. They wouldn't stop yelling and berating each other, especially Lorena. Before I had time to come up with alternatives for their behavior, I found myself starting to yell at the top of my lungs. "You need to quit, and I mean now!"

Both Lorena and Manuel were visibly startled by my outburst, but so was I. I had never before, nor have I since, yelled at any of my clients or associates like I did that day with Lorena and Manuel. Once we all stopped, I explained to them very calmly and quietly that they were terrorizing their two little children by fighting loudly and constantly like that.

After that day things got much better for them. Lorena and Manuel apparently gave what I said some thought and were able to iron out their differences using "indoor voices" and compromising, when before they just did not care what the other had to say. In addition, Lorena and Manuel figured out other ways to vent their differences. I was proud of them. And their kids were a lot happier. About three months after the screaming episode, Lorena and Manuel stopped in to see me while I was still at the Glendale office. They were all doing fine. What a relief, and the true proof of success was that no more CPS reports were called on them.

17

Teresa Garcia, Maria, Dirty Houses, and Dads

Teresa was the maternal aunt to a girl, Maria, who had witnessed as a young child her mom's murder by a boyfriend. Mom was in her early thirties, and Maria was ten or so, when the murder took place. The advantage of the child being older was that Maria was provided more intensive therapy than would be provided to a toddler. The aunt became Maria's guardian for seven years. Then Maria started to act up. It wasn't a major deal, just the usual kind of teen conflicts: Maria violated her curfew a few times. She sometimes slacked at chores. I was of the opinion that the aunt was overly paranoid because of what had happened to Maria's mom.

Maria was seventeen and a half years of age. Maria was responsible enough and had a steady boyfriend, but the relationship became a problem between Maria and her aunt, so the child went to stay at her adult sister's house. Then I entered the picture. The guardian ad litem had filed a private petition since Maria was no longer staying at Aunt Teresa's house. I talked to the aunt and headed for the adult sibling's house to talk with Maria and her sister.

Maria's sister and her husband lived in an impressive, gorgeous house located in a wonderful neighborhood. The adult sibling was twenty-one and had two little babies. I assumed Maria's sibling had either married a man from a rich family or perhaps someone older than herself. Maria's sibling did not work.

When I arrived at the sibling's house, I discovered that Maria was no longer staying there. My initial response was "Uh oh. Perhaps we do have a problem here after all." Maria was staying at her boyfriend's house, allegedly. The sibling said that she and Aunt Teresa did not get along.

The adult sibling painted an unflattering picture of Maria and her boyfriend, which didn't help. In my mind, I was already preparing for the worst possible scenario: that Maria was with some younger version of Mom's boyfriend, the murderer.

I called the phone number the sibling had given me for Maria and went to the address Maria provided. I was expecting Maria to give me a phony address and try to jerk me around, but that was the farthest from the truth. Maria herself answered the door when I arrived. She was a remarkably clean-cut teenager, not rough around the edges at all. The house was a nice house in an established neighborhood of Glendale, a very respectable neighborhood. When I arrived, Maria was babysitting her boyfriend's baby sibling.

The one-year-old was a serene, well-cared-for tot. She and Maria interacted well together. It was easy to see that Maria was far from wild. She was soft spoken and patient by nature. As I continued to talk to Maria, I discovered that Maria had moved in with her boyfriend and his family. They were not living alone or with other teens.

The house was immaculately clean. CPS staff recognize that our job is not so much about surface judgments. But there is a correlation between the condition of a house that, to an extent, reflects the state of a person's mind. Our worst cases usually occur in houses in states of total neglect or chaos: filthy and/or uninhabitable. There is a correspondence between the two. It makes me thankful I grew up in one of the clean houses; I repeated the same standards later in life, though I was quite a messy teenager. When talking about dirty houses, I am not referring to a pile of clutter here or there or an overcrowded room with ugly furniture. I am specifically referring to a house where trash is overflowing for endless miles, a house where dirty dishes have been piled in the sink for so long that the food is plastered to the dishes. Some dirty homes smell like urine is imbedded permanently in the carpets (although I've also heard that meth smells like urine, so who knows which is which?).

As an agency, we do not necessarily remove children because a house is dirty; we do not remove kids based on that alone. We remove kids if the dirty house is a safety threat to the child, for example if dog feces covered the carpet along with broken glass, and the child was a crawling baby or young toddler. That glass could cut and hurt a little child who doesn't know better than to put it in his or her mouth or isn't old enough to avoid stepping on the glass. Feces could poison a child, especially a baby or a toddler, who doesn't know better and puts any in his or her mouth.

It may sound unbelievable to you that a house could be so filthy. I had been in several houses that were that bad. Some were roach infested. Remember Henry and Elsa Potter and their daughter Katie from a few chapters ago? Their house fit this category. On the other hand, a spotless house does not ensure child abuse won't take place. It just happens a lot more in the filthy houses.

In any case, I was reassured to find that where Maria was staying was nicely furnished, spotless, and in a nice family neighborhood. Maria and I sat and talked. I brought up her mother's death a little reluctantly. I did not want to bum Maria out, but I needed to know something about her feelings, as well as her coping skills, since that fateful event. I apologized for bringing it up. Maria briefly and in a poised fashion, considering her youth, told me that Mom had not been with biological Dad for a long time. Mom had met some guy who was into the wrong things, including drugs. Mom and the boyfriend had been together for three years or so. Plenty of domestic violence was splattered here and there, right up until the grand finale.

Mom had started out as a good mom, but after the boyfriend, everything took a quick detour south. Apparently, Maria and her older sister had begged Mom to break up with the guy. Their mother never stood a chance. One day in the heat of the moment, it was all over forever.

I asked Maria how she coped after the murder. Maria was thankful for having gone to therapy to talk about the trauma. The loss still hurt a lot, but Maria said she was also glad not to have to suffer the effects of witnessing domestic violence any longer. Maria's sister had told me that Maria's boyfriend was aggressive, so I naturally wanted to specifically address that. In CPS, we're all too keenly aware that the very horrible elements children are subjected to often repeat when those CPS kids become parents. Old habits die hard.

I asked Maria about her boyfriend and what kind of relationship they had. What kind of plans did they have for the future, if any? (I had to chuckle at the irony in my own life here. When I was growing up, my parents were emphatic that "a life without planning means you will wind up nowhere." While I was a carefree youth and thought that was a bunch of hogwash, as a middle-aged adult I value that lesson keenly. My only regret was that I did not see the reality of that way of thinking earlier on.)

Anyway, Maria's reply reassured me. She was graduating high school in a month and a half. She was going to enroll in nursing school. That is a lucrative and honorable profession, I thought. Maria's boyfriend's dad worked at one of the local colleges, and he was helping her be admitted into the college where he worked. Maria had great grades. In her final semester, she only had to take half a load of courses instead of a full load. Her boyfriend had already finished high school, had a job, and was getting into a trade profession. The boyfriend was about two years older than Maria. He had been at his job for one year and was doing well. The couple had met because of mutual friends. They were churchgoers. I could see no bad influences or dangers from my end.

I asked Maria what had happened with her aunt. I wanted to hear her version in case it differed greatly from what the aunt said.

Often, individual versions did differ tremendously. (All I could say in the long run was that the truth usually rested somewhere between both versions.) Maria claimed she still saw her aunt on a regular basis and loved her dearly. Aunt Teresa was worrying over the situation, but nothing bad was going on. I thought, *Yes, and Maria's sister is also worrying over the situation. And to top it off, Maria's sister and Aunt Teresa are no longer on speaking terms!* Teresa was mostly nervous because of what had happened to Teresa's own sister, Maria's mom.

Maria volunteered info about her dad as well. She said that she was angry at her father for a number of years but that she had been back in touch with him in the last three years; they had become much closer. I was thrilled to hear that. Maria's sister had a different dad. Maria was her father's only child. Maria commented that her mother had brainwashed her against her father, and she didn't know that he did want to be involved in her life. I was to find out later that he did seek custody of Maria, in fact, before and after Mom's murder.

That became a real sore spot with me, when moms or relatives tried to prohibit the children's fathers from seeing their own children or sharing custody. Why was it okay to have a child with someone and then deny the person's existence? If a woman only wants a sperm donor, go to a sperm bank. It's even worse when a woman has a child just to collect welfare or child support. That is such a damaging way to think; no wonder the child is bound to turn out screwed up. A child is always a blessing from God, whom both parents should want to and be able to provide for.

(It does work both ways. It's sad to know there are bum guys out there who merely reproduce and are unable or unwilling to help support their children. It is sad and scary to visualize a world when a parent or both parents lack responsibility to care for their child. Add methamphetamine to the mix and we might expect a nation void of emotion, half full of zombies. Gulp.)

I figured Maria might not be thrilled, but now was the time

to bring it up: how about if she were to stay at Dad's just until she graduated the end of May? It would only be for two months. Or, as an alternate plan, we could make Dad the safety monitor. She could stay at both houses, but then Dad could check on Maria to ensure her well-being. Maria agreed, especially after I emphasized that my motivation was to get the guardian ad litem to drop the petition in court. This kind of plan would make it more likely to have the petition dropped. So Maria called and explained in Spanish to her dad what she and I had discussed. She told her dad that I needed to stop over and bring the paperwork and to briefly see his place. After collecting my interpreter, I went over. I made sure a background check was already done. Maria's dad confirmed what Maria had told me in my interview with her: he did want custody and Maria did come and spend nights on a semiregular basis.

I asked Maria's dad if he had ever met Maria's boyfriend. The dad replied that he had met the boyfriend, and the young man seemed okay. I answered, "Okay, but if you ever see any signs involving abuse of any sort between the two of them, please do intervene as her father." I went on to say that we did not want to see a reenactment of Mom's violent domestic lifestyle filter into Maria's lifestyle down the road, especially since Maria had witnessed that domestic violence firsthand.

This thought appeared to be a revelation to Maria's dad. His eyes lit up while he contemplated the full scope of events, almost as if that comment had turned on a light switch in his brain. His demeanor went from friendly to somber, and he assured me he would do just that. He had already missed a good part of Maria's childhood because Mom and Teresa kept him at arm's length. Now that he really was trying to play the role of father, he wanted the responsibility for being Maria's emotional protection too.

I went back to the aunt to update her on the petition developments. At first, she seemed not to believe that this dad wanted his child. I insisted that he did and that he was entitled to have her in his custody, especially since Maria wanted the same.

The aunt felt better about that than if Maria were to stay only at the boyfriend's. By the time we were done conversing, Teresa was thankful to hear a thread of stability did exist for Maria. Teresa confessed before I left that yes, Maria did still call and come by on a regular basis. Teresa was fearful about her sister's untimely death and how that fate might impact Maria in the future.

When the case went to court, I told the attorney general (AG) that the state's position was to dismiss the dependency. I am not sure if the AG agreed and did not care. I was going to make sure my position was heard. I was made aware that the guardian ad litem received $2,000 for each petition he filed and that this particular GAL was notorious for filing many such petitions and making a good income from it.

Chris, the GAL, acted indignant about the situation, but I had my way. How? Because I told Maria and her dad that the best way to get the case dismissed was for the two of them to show up to court together. Seeing is believing. I had a feeling Maria might wig out, but no. When the day came, she and her dad appeared together: happy, confident, and natural. They were loving and close to each other, which was apparent to even a stranger. The judge picked up on that and dismissed the case. It wasn't a put-on show; the affection and bond between daughter and Dad was real.

I was elated over another happy ending. In CPS, there are far too few happy endings. Sorry, Chris. I'll take another win when I can!

18

Dana Christian

Dana Christian's story was a peculiar one. (Aren't they all?) Dana was a child who had hurt her sibling, according to the mom. The sibling, Lindy, was an autistic child. Dana was dragging Lindy along the carpet, which made long scratches on Lindy's back. When I went to conduct the investigation, the mom, Kristy, showed me the injuries Lindy had sustained a week previously. She'd stored pictures on her digital camera. Kristy had waited until Lindy healed before calling CPS. Kristy's reasoning was that she didn't want anyone to think she had committed physical abuse against Lindy. The family had just moved to Arizona from Ohio, and Lindy did not have the communication skills to explain what had really happened.

I told Kristy that I would speak to Dana about the incident. Dana was upstairs in her room at the time. I knocked on the door, introduced myself, stepped inside the room, and closed the door. I could tell by Dana's reaction when I asked what had happened to Lindy that she was indeed responsible for the incident. Dana hung her head low and confessed to doing it in a trembling voice. I could feel the guilt radiating from her. Dana said that she hadn't meant to do it, that "she was bad and didn't deserve this family." Dana was twelve years old and jealous of Lindy. She wanted Mom all to herself.

I reviewed Dana's history. It looked really bleak. Dana had been sexually abused as a baby. Now Dana was given to fits of violence. She had no knowledge of what had happened to her as an infant, but obviously, deep inside, she sensed on that much deeper level the kind of horror that had afflicted her before her removal from her own biological parents. So Dana reacted the injustice done to her by having periodic violent episodes. Unsure where to take this, CPS, served a ninety-day voluntary; Dana came into our care for three months. We put her into a mental health facility on a temporary basis to assist Dana and Mom.

The adoptive mom planned to move back to Ohio with the other kids. When they were resituated in Ohio, Kristy would fly back for Dana. First, she would line up a good therapeutic placement for Dana back in Ohio. Dana missed her family, to the point I was afraid she would attempt to kill herself. Though workers are only required to see our kids once monthly, I drove weekly to Scottsdale to visit her and take her to eat at McDonald's, assuring Dana that Mom would come back for her.

Kristy had confessed to me before moving that the real reason she had moved to Arizona was that Kristy had found out that Michael, her husband of many years, had cheated on her with some sleazy stripper. Kristy was hurt beyond belief. So she moved. Kristy had picked Arizona because she had a few local relatives: a daughter, and the other might have been an aunt. All the while, Michael was begging Kristy and the kids to return. Michael had had an executive position with a company and got so sick after they left that he lost his job. I was actually glad that Kristy and her husband made up and started the long ride back to Ohio together. He flew out to help her.

Dana was sure that her family had officially deserted her and that "she was no good." I kept encouraging Dana and told her that they just couldn't have Dana drive with them cooped up in the car for three whole days. The three months seemed like forever for Dana and me. On a sweet day close to Christmas, I was able to arrange a plane ticket for Dana. I said to her, "See? Didn't I tell you your family really wants you, to just hang in there and believe it will happen?" Before going to the airport, we went to Walgreens to get Dana's prescription filled. It was crucial that Dana take something for the long plane ride and to tide her over when she first got back to Ohio. Naturally, nothing went smoothly. Walgreens gave me a hard time. I forget what the problem was, but I kept looking at the clock. I had the store call our district CMDP insurance (comprehensive medical dental plan) through AHCCS.

Walgreens said it would take an extra hour, or something to that effect. I was virtually screaming that the sick little girl had to catch a plane. Finally they filled her prescription. We raced to the airport. Luckily, it was the middle of day, and there was no traffic for a change. We hooked up with Kristy while waiting in line at the airport. It was worth a million dollars to see Dana's face when she got to the airport and saw Kristy.

On one of our last visits together, I thought of little Dana, a sweet girl who was religious, trying to sort her troubled life out in her head. I did not know how to broach the truth of her background without revealing all. She did want answers but was not ready for the full-blown truth. I am not a therapist who could walk her through it all. But I looked at her squarely and remarked, "Dana, one day the truth will not enslave you as it does now. One day the truth will, instead, set you free. Please remember that and know that."

I did not, in fact, know that myself. I merely prayed that it would be that way. That was what Dana wanted, for the truth to set her free. Dana looked at me quizzically but as if she did understand what I was trying to convey to her on some level. And silence can sometimes hold more truth than words do. Kristy went back to Ohio with Dana, and, while Dana did experience a few minor incidents, she did a lot better, at least for the time being. It was a good start.

19

Annette Macias

Annette's mom, Andrea, and her aunt called CPS on Annette. Mom was a lovely young adult, with long, dark, wavy hair, a tiny upturned nose, big eyes, and thick lips. She was very slender, to the point of fragile, and graceful. Annette had two boys, ages one and three. Annette would leave them with her mom, but she went out one time too often. Grandma had had it. Maybe it wasn't because Andrea was angry. It could have been because Andrea had had cancer and was recovering. Annette's dad, Andrea's ex-husband, had died recently. There was a lot of stress.

The boys' dad was in prison. Annette had left him because his violent nature had come out, and Annette did not want any part of it. One of the children, the elder one, had special needs and was hypersensitive. He would sometimes start screaming out of the clear blue. He might have had a form of autism.

Annette was in tears when I appeared for the interview. She did take care of her boys and wanted to continue; she just needed help and support. "They are all I have" were Annette's words. Annette could not understand why her mother and aunt were so hard on her.

The little boys were really attached to Annette. She loved them, but as a too-young mom on her own, it was just too much for her to care for them. They were behind on their immunizations.

So Annette had to see about that before she could get them into daycare, which CPS could provide for free for six months, as long as the daycare was affiliated with the Department of Economic Security (DES). Once the children were in daycare, Annette could get a job. Sad to say, Annette was never able to get to that stage of the game. We wound up having to file a dependency on Annette's children.

Andrea had job security and a clean background. She had known her share of grief; her son was incarcerated for I forget how many years, plus the recent passing of Annette's dad and now this conflict with Annette and the kids.

Annette, in her hysteria over what was happening, chose to give up and disappear at the time of the dependency. Annette's mom, in the meantime, moved. While I believe Annette wound up losing all her rights to the kids, I am happy to say that at some point she found out where the kids and her mom had moved to and started going around again, in a good way.

When it comes to family, when there is no physical abuse or violence or destruction of property, families need to stay glued together and try to salvage whatever they can for the sake of the children and for some support among themselves. This is part of what we call family-based strength.

20

Octavia Ruiz and Little Jose

Jose was a charming little guy, five years old. He was very slight in stature, with big brown eyes and short dark hair. I went to see him at his elementary school. He was in kindergarten. The report stated that Mom had hit him and left marks, and there was a police report. (Technically, any cases of physical abuse that are noted at a school will generally involve the police taking pictures of the injuries. This is pretty standard policy, no matter what school it is.) In the comments on the CPS report, Jose said that he was afraid of Octavia. Octavia was Jose's legal guardian. Jose's mom had died from a hard life, for lack of a better diagnosis. Did it involve drugs? Most certainly it did. Meth is a killer, and if I have not convinced you of that, there are many cases of moms and dads who die in the prime of their lives due to the rampages of that lifestyle. The ones who live appear at age thirty more as if they were fifty-five years old or older if they have used heavily.

Jose's biological mother knew she was dying, and she asked Octavia if she would be willing to take Jose in and care for him until he reached the age of majority. I can't recall if Octavia and Jose's mom were ex-neighbors, because they did not hang in the same circles. In any case, Octavia wanted to take care of Jose and agreed to do just that, without hesitation. Jose had two sisters who lived elsewhere. Jose and his sisters did get together from time to time. This delighted me as the case manager. That is sometimes the worse impact separations have. Poor little children are not only are minus their parents but also without their biological siblings. (I was often terribly concerned during the short time I spent in the adoptions unit later on about whether the adoptive parents would truly maintain sibling contact between kids or if they were only paying lip service. Once the adoption was final, there was no more CPS intervention to check and ensure that children were maintaining contact with siblings.) Everyone gets busy and caught up in their own lives.

When I saw Jose at his school, he said that he was afraid when Mom hit him. I retorted, "I am going to go talk to your mom and make sure she never hits you again. If she ever does, you must tell your teacher, and I will take care of the problem. I will not let her continue to hit you. That goes for this year, next year, and so on." I asked Jose if he could remember all that, and he said he could. Jose appeared very happy at my words, like a load had been lifted off his back. Jose also explained that he did love his mom and he did love living with her. Nonetheless, the little boy relaxed and thanked me. Then he asked if he could draw me a picture. I said, "Sure, draw it now. I'll wait." It was drawn all in blue, and it had a little stick figure in it with a path and a house.

Jose asked that I write my name, Bea, on it and the word *secret*. I wrote the words on his picture with a touch of amusement. I kept that picture for the ten years I worked at CPS and hung it on my wall at work. Many CPS workers hang up the pictures that their little angels draw them. Contrary to the general heartlessness that the general public claims of us, not only do workers hang these pictures up, we try to soothe the kids the best we can. We ensure they are fed when they are hungry; we change their clothes when needed and do other small acts to show they are cared about. It sometimes affect us more than the parents to walk in on horrible conditions, when parents are oblivious or uncaring about the effect they have on their children. Everyone—the media, the court, even politicians—always prefers to blame monstrosities visited on children on CPS. Why didn't we do something faster? Why didn't we remove the children sooner? Why didn't we return the children sooner? It was never the parents' fault that a kid died, always CPS's fault.

I went to Octavia's house, fuming when I thought of the tiny soul who'd lost his mom and sisters, everything he knew, now having to take beatings from a guardian whose job was to protect and love him. Octavia presented herself as friendly when I introduced myself. (I went unannounced the first time, as is CPS policy. Octavia worked, but I had left a business card. She called, and we were able to arrange a meeting time.) Octavia showed me Jose's cheerful bedroom. The room contained a SpongeBob computer and SpongeBob TV. His bed had a SpongeBob comforter and pillow. (I later bought a SpongeBob TV, comforter, and pillow myself for a little boy whom I wanted to comfort, but that is another subject and he was not a CPS case.) The room was cute and cheerful.

I got right to the point and told Octavia I was going to substantiate child abuse, that I had to, based upon the police report and Jose's account of the incident. Octavia broke down crying, I believe out of true regret, or was she feeling shame? This was the first case I was substantiating abuse on. I did feel uncomfortable about substantiating the report, but not enough to stop me from doing so. After all, it was part of my job.

Octavia told me she loved Jose and did not want him taken away. I responded that I was not going to take him away from her. I added that I felt they needed counseling. After all, he was a tot who lost his mother; he needed to deal with that death and work it out. Octavia felt badly that she had been hard on him. I told her the counselor could help identify other disciplinary practices. She was very open to doing what it took to keep Jose happy and healthy.

I went back to the school a few months later to see Jose. He was doing great! Though he'd appeared way too serious the first time I met him, this time he showed genuine happiness, and there was a certain carefree manner about him that he did not seem to possess originally. No more sadness prevailed. Jose told me that his mom did not hit him anymore. I told him, "Good. She better not, or she will have me to deal with."

I felt I did my job properly on this case. I made Mom feel bad about what she did to a little boy who had already lived through enough trauma. I brought out Mom's feelings of love for the child with compassion instead of exasperation. Octavia had become side-tracked by too much else to realize the amount of love Jose was so in need of, which was more than she was giving. It was also past conditioning on her part. I understood that. She was raised that to "spare the rod is to spoil the child." However, sometimes kindness and gentle words go much further and are needed so much more.

All Octavia needed to do was focus on Jose's needs and watch him blossom and grow. It was worth it, too, for Octavia really loved little Jose, and he really loved her.

21

Gloria Cilanto

The police called in a report on Gloria. The mom had left her little girls unattended at a store; luckily, the store owner watched them until her return. However, when I contacted the source, the officer who had reported the incident said the situation turned out to be other than the way it originally appeared to be. Apparently the store owner was Gloria's boyfriend. Also, Gloria had reappeared within half an hour of her departure from the girls. At that point I did not feel much trepidation over the matter. Yet it was my job to conduct the investigation.

According to CPS policy, we attempt to touch base with the source first. If it is a professional source—police, hospital, social worker, therapist, school—we give it more weight. Sometimes when the source is relatives, ulterior motives are involved. And while we do investigate anonymous reports, sometimes those reports are the farthest from the truth. What we try to emphasize to the general public is that the source always remains confidential. We do not disclose that information. So if a person is holding back from calling CPS, we encourage them not to hold back due to fear of being discovered. It is better to try to save a child, if you feel that child's safety is endangered. Anyway, despite what the police explained, I still had to complete my investigation and offer services.

Gloria was candid with me. She said she would never jeopardize her children's safety. Her eldest daughter had gone to stay with a maternal aunt and lived far enough away that it was a hardship for Gloria. Gloria wanted to get her eldest daughter, Moriah, back home. Moriah was then fourteen. Gloria was staying at the Motel 6, I think the one near Bell Road in North Phoenix. She said her husband had just split on her, which was how she wound up at the motel. Gloria said he stole $1,500 from her, plus her computer. Prior to that, Gloria had worked a solid year at a local company and had a reference on letterhead. I called and verified the information. In addition to working, Gloria was also going to school online part-time before the ex stole her computer. Naturally, I felt sorry for her. Here was a mother who was working and trying hard to better herself.

When I asked about Gloria's upbringing, she said it was the worst. Her father had sexually abused Gloria's one sister and went to prison for it. Luckily, he did not do anything to Gloria, maybe because she was the baby in the family. *Or maybe she doesn't remember if there was abuse*, I thought to myself. Gloria had a previous history of drugs from before she got married, worked, and took classes. That made sense. How could someone on drugs accomplish working and going to school, along with taking care of two little girls? Drug people never are able to accomplish anything except for their rap that only they believe. Also, Gloria was always dressed in business clothes and had a good complexion. She talked very clearly and made sense; there was no obvious sign of drug usage. Her place and her children were clean, and the children were well fed.

I surmised that one of Gloria's big faults was that she was always trying to help others. I told her not to do so, at least not until she could get back on her own two feet. After the interview, I planned to give her services, but Gloria just sort of disappeared. *Not a good sign*, I thought.

However, three months later I received a call from Gloria. She was staying with her kids at a Vista Colinas homeless shelter in the

Sunnyslope part of North Phoenix. I went to see her and the kids; the shelter had given Gloria her own apartment and provided free daycare. The shelter would let families stay three to six months. I was proud of Gloria that she had accomplished all this on her own. It was around Christmas in 2006, so I dropped off some presents for the girls. I was delighted to see Gloria on her own, functioning well and showing a sense of capability.

About six months later I received another report on Gloria. The report said Gloria was working at a storage place and lived on the premises. Gloria had been there at least several months and was doing well. Then suddenly Gloria was taking off from work all the time and lost her job. It was rumored she went back to the use of meth.

I went out to conduct an interview, but Gloria had already vanished. I was unable to catch up with Gloria but figured the next worker would. Then, unfortunately, on February 6, 2008, Gloria resurfaced. She was busted on warrants, and someone else was assigned the case. The assigned CPS worker at that time had a dependency petition on Gloria's two little girls, Mary and Lily. There was also mention of sexual abuse. In addition, the other daughter, Moriah, now sixteen, had come back in the picture and was pregnant with her first child. Gloria tracked me down, but I explained that I was no longer on her case anymore, nor could I talk when she called me, as I had just removed a child on another case who was sitting literally at my desk. I was working actively on that particular case at the time of her call.

Sadly, one thing can be said for sure: as far as Gloria and her family, the cycle of abuse continues.

22

Gayle Lombard

Gayle's CPS report was about the boyfriend sexually abusing her thirteen-year-old. Gayle, when she found out, went to the police, and they arrested him. In the meantime, Gayle moved out of the apartment she shared with the boyfriend into the house where her sister lived. She didn't want to be around when her ex got out of jail.

I liked Gayle and felt sorry for her. Some women would have gone along with the situation

out of a false sense of loyalty or denial. Gayle showed she loved her child by doing the right thing. She did not choose the easy path but the right one. She also probably lost her source of income in the process. But at least she had principles; she stood up for and cared about her two kids. Whether she knew how to make good choices in men or not, she had a sense of conscience about doing the right thing. Hopefully the counseling we provided helped Gayle deal with whatever guilt or frustration she might have been feeling to prevent her from repeating a similar mistake in the future.

23

Carrie Ambrosia

Carrie was my only real high-profile case. She was on the news because her four-year-old child was found wandering on a busy street. I believe it was Indian School, around or near Grand Avenue, if memory serves me. It happened after sundown. The worst part was that it had actually happened once before, and recently. Because of that, the police decided to charge Carrie with child abuse.

When I went to the residence to do the interview, part of me was thinking that I was chosen because I always achieved my response time when a lot of other CPS workers barely did. I noticed that the girls were very nice and cute. They seemed happy and did not show any obvious signs of neglect. The house was neat, not dumpy at all. It was quite different than what I'd expected to find. The little four-year-old, Marina, seemed like an adventurous and devious little monkey, with no inherent fear. When we held our team decision-making meeting, I was advised by higher-ups before the meeting that my decision would be to do an in-home dependency. That way, we wouldn't remove the kids, but the "running off" safety risk could be intensely addressed.

Leading up to the chain of events, Carrie had been depressed because she and her boyfriend had broken up. In addition to that, she had problems with both dads of her two kids. One had deserted them and was nowhere to be found; the other worked steadily but was behind on his child support. I am not particularly fond of deadbeat fathers and felt payment would help save the state budget from offering assistance, so I told Family Preservation to help Mom contact child support to get Dad to catch up with his obligations.

The in-home unit was not all that fond of me, to put it mildly. I think they foresaw me as a wishy-washy, overly friendly person, goofy and spacey at times. Who knows? Maybe their assessment of me wasn't totally incorrect. I had an abnormally friendly air with my clients for the most part. My motivation was that a lot of them had hard lives, and I thought maybe I could reach them by breaking the ice and helping them retract their defensive guards. Isn't that a good way to reach people, especially ones in bad situations who are stressed? (Also, I think I was protecting myself. The parents would be less likely to want to harm or murder someone who seemed less threatening than an abrasive worker, if it came down to that.)

That way of thinking doesn't make my way right, although it seemed to work sufficiently for me in a number of cases. But my ideology differed greatly from that of the in-home unit. I was not trying to go easy on Carrie. I was just trying to be friendly in order to understand what led up to these events and to convey in a friendly but strong way that it "doesn't work like that." Not to say the in-home unit went in and badgered her, but I saw her nervousness was much more pronounced in their presence. I was wondering if that could predispose the person to and set her up for failure? Who knows?

I can say that most of my clients really liked me while I worked in investigations, to my knowledge, and I was very committed to helping them on a deep level, especially for their kids' welfare. Many of them still copped out, but at least we had better dealings along the way. I would also try to convey that I was not playing the role of adversary. We were actually teammates, whether we wanted to be or not, thrown together to come up with a game plan that would hopefully mean a win for all involved. The win would mean the parents and kids stayed together or reunified and corrected the problem, whatever it might entail. And if anything did go haywire, the case manager, I reminded them, was the first person the media would point fingers at. So if my teammates suffered a loss, so did I. Their loss was greater, however, not to mention their kids' loss.

Anyway, I sensed the fear that Carrie exuded and felt the in-home unit did make it harder on her. Yet, to be objective, those at the TDM meeting speculated about what would possess a four-year-old to want to wander off the way this child had? Most four-year-olds do not do that; they stay close to Mommy. If they do wander, it is usually a short distance. The child was over a mile or so from where they lived when she was found.

I remember being four and wandering off from my mom at the grocery store a little. The minute I didn't see my mom and couldn't find her, I broke down, sobbing, "Mommy, Mommy," until an adult came to my aid and they located her. In that short time, I thought my heart was going to break, that I had lost my mommy forever. What would I do? But here, on the other hand, was a little four-year-old who had wandered perhaps as much as a mile, without being fazed by it and not missing her mother. She was on a very busy street, not crying, not seeming afraid.

When I interviewed Marina, she was charming and expressive, much like her older sister, only a tad more dramatic. She was lapping up the extra attention she had gained through her actions, as if proud of them. In the long run, I was glad the in-home unit took over. Maybe they had extra insights that an investigator did not have the time to formulate or strategize over.

After I transferred and worked in ongoing for six years, I saw how deceptive people really could be. Yet, once in a blue moon, I'd see a person triumph, moving from the bottom of the barrel to the top of the mountain through effort, love of their child, and insight gained (known as behavioral changes made). And I would say that that is nothing short of a miracle. When parents become truly righteous and self-aware for the sake of their loved little child, that's what any social worker lives in hope of seeing, especially when it involves innocent children.

In our job, we can also see that when a little kid is way too friendly and casual, it might not be a good sign and could possibly indicate neglect, even if unintentional. Likewise, when an adult becomes wrapped up in sticky situations with the wrong people and there are children involved, that can really spell trouble in the long run: situations of neglect and/or worse just waiting to occur. Like Mom used to say, "We are known by the company we keep."

Luckily Marina was not run over in that traffic; it was a second (maybe last) chance for Carrie with her children.

24

Judith Robles

Judith Robles was involved in a sex abuse case. Mom's boyfriend abused the daughter, Gania. I interviewed Judith's six kids at school. Then I went to see Judith. Judith defended her boyfriend, a common jailbird Judith had met at the complex where she used to live. Judith's reasoning was that if Gania had had relations with Michael, she would have screamed in pain, as Michael was a big guy. Gania was very petite and very thin.

I took all the information and then leveled with Judith. I said that whether Michael had truly done the act with Gania or not, the point was that Judith did not believe her daughter or defend her. I explained that because of that, she had failed to protect Gania. Many parents put the spouse or boyfriend first, even at the risk of the child's safety. I haven't had the best relationships in the world myself either, but I would draw the line when it came to endangering my kid. I would probably try to kill the perp instead of defend him! Maybe some of these parents just were blind to the facts, and it was easier to pretend like nothing was happening and leave it at that, without rocking the status quo. Maybe it was their bad past conditioning.

I explained to Judith that we would either need a 24-7 safety monitor or I would have to file a dependency petition, especially because the allegations concerned sexual abuse. The temporary outcome was that all the kids except for Joshua were going to stay with Grandma. Judith wasn't thrilled about it, but I told her she did not have much choice. It was the only other option, as a matter of fact.

Judith was rather coldhearted and showed it in her attitude toward Gania. Judith wanted Gania to go back to her dad's rather than staying at Grandma's house. Judith told Harrison, the dad, this, and Harrison called Grandma, demanding Gania return immediately to him and threatening to come from California to pick Gania up. The terrified grandma then called me. She explained that right after the incident between Michael and Gania, Judith had sent Gania to her dad's. Instead of believing his child and comforting her through the bad times, Harrison wound up beating her instead. Grandma told Harrison she wouldn't press charges if Gania could come stay with her. Now this …

I asked the grandmother if she had Harrison's number, which she gave to me. While Grandma Valerie was scared of Harrison—there was no doubt about that—she also told me that Harrison was on parole. Who knew for what. One could only imagine. Without further ado, I called Harrison and got his voice message. I left Harrison a threatening message to that effect that "I'm with CPS, and you better leave Gania alone or I will pursue filing a police report against you for beating her, as well as call in a CPS report on you in your area. And if that isn't enough, I could throw in a call to your parole officer, because I am guessing you are violating your parole."

I also mentioned to him that I had given Valerie directions to call the police if Harrison were to appear on her premises. I left my phone number in case he preferred to call me back and discuss it. Surprisingly, he did not call back, nor did Valerie hear anymore from him after my phone call. (I am being sarcastic. I knew darn well he would lay off. I had him sized up accurately: a loser punk who would try to pull his stuff on whomever he could intimidate.)

Valerie was relieved that problem was taken care of. She

asked what was next. I told her that since a safety monitor plan is temporary, her best bet would to be to file for guardianship of the kids. In the meantime, Michael did not cooperate with taking the polygraph. Another surprise, right? The police detective told me she felt Gania was totally convincing, that she had no doubt that the child wasn't trying to make up some story. The bad thing was that they had no forensic evidence to nail Michael with, nor could they force Michael to take the polygraph.

Although I believed Gania, I did not substantiate the sex abuse charge at the time. I later realized I had failed to protect Gania and attempted to change all that. I was not clear about what made substantiation charges stick and what didn't. I was further confused by having to go through a review committee, who determines whether a worker has met the critieria for making substantiation charges stick. If you don't word the substantiation part in such and such a way, the review committee won't accept it. On a few of my cases, I had to keep submitting my substantiation findings over and over. It wouldn't be such a big deal, but when you are bombarded with reports and phones ringing off the hook, with major crises in the making on both closed and open cases, it was just another bone to add to the heap of all your other skeletons. There are many of them, and they do not stay in the closet.

When I had sent Judith the original unsubstantiated letter, she proceeded to rub it in by saying to Grandma, " I told you Michael was innocent." Valerie was devastated; therefore, I wrote a letter saying that I felt that because Michael did not take the polygraph, that exemplified a state of guilt, though I did not have the legal proof, so I couldn't get him convicted. There was little I could do about it. I added that if there were any way Valerie or Judith could convince Michael to take the polygraph, that would be the best outcome in the situation. Naturally, Michael wasn't going to, but at least he and Judith shut up.

Gania was having a problem at school at the time, fighting with another girl. I told Gania that fighting is not good. I believed she was mad at Michael, her mom, and her dad, but I knew that fighting someone else was not going to help her address those issues.

Gania said, "No. It's because the girl keeps picking on me."

"Fine. Then wear a sign that says 'I refuse to fight anymore for any reason.' Do what it takes to hold off, Gania," I replied. I got a smile out of her when I said that. I doubt Gania even entertained the idea of wearing such a sign, but I heard of no further incidents of her fighting after that. Way to go, Gania. You are one smart girl to be reckoned with!

Valerie had recently received guardianship for the girls. Harrison and Joshua had moved to the Midwest with Mom. I called Gia's dad in Iowa (she was another child of Mom's, living with her dad) to make sure that Gia's dad felt the situation of the boys being with Judith was appropriate. Mr. Barristo had never been involved with CPS; he had a clean record. He seemed to be able to offer a good but objective opinion and family support, as well. After having Gia with Judith, Mr. Barristo had then moved away to Iowa, got married, and was very steady since. He said he would be happy to watch out for the boys. The boys were going to come visit Gia, their baby sister, on a regular basis. When I asked Mr. Barristo if he knew if Michael was still in Judith's life, he said he did not believe so, so that was a good sign.

Mr. Barristo said he would definitely keep Michael away from Gia if Michael were still involved and keep CPS informed if there were any concerns. Mr. Barristo was aware of what had happened with Gania; he'd found out not from Valerie but from Judith herself because Judith did not want Gania or any of her other kids to stay with Grandma. So apparently she had confided in Mr. Barristo. Mr. Barristo was not taken in by Judith's account of the situation, however. He said he knew Judith too well for that. In good faith, he was hoping that by moving to the Midwest, maybe Judith would get a clean start and do better by starting over.

Before the grand finale, when Judith moved with Joshua and Isaac, family court had contacted me for my opinion regarding the boys. Valerie was trying to get guardianship of Isaac and Joshua as well as for Gania and her older sister Victoria. Though I suspected the boys would be better off with Valerie, nonetheless, there were other considerations. The boys were much closer to their mom than Gania was, and, based upon my interviews with the boys at school, neither Michael or anybody else had ever attempted sexually inappropriate behavior with them. Therefore, there were no safety risks that I knew of that would prohibit the boys from being with Mom, even if she wasn't the best mother known to mankind. The boys were so attached to her, and, based upon my interview with them, I could clearly see that Judith had very different and much better dynamics with her sons than with her girls.

I tried to convey this to the court in a diplomatic and neutral way. While the boys were not quite teenagers, they were far from being little toddlers, which was another point in their favor, as far as wanting to be with their mom. The safety risks with older kids is much less than that of toddlers and babies. In the end, Isaac and Joshua were allowed to go with their mom and were quite happy. Especially with Mr. Barristo's family there as a normal extended family, the boys would have every reason to grow up to be normal, well-adjusted young men.

The boys did advise me during our interview that Michael used to preach to them about how bad jail was. So that was a good thing. Lastly, unlike many of our other "average parents," Mom had never been in jail, did not have a drug problem, and for a number of years had held a rather good job with the state of Arizona, which was true right until her departure. So possibly there was hope for Judith too. Again, we turned to family-based strengths to help this family succeed.

25

Elijah and Danielle Morisa

Danielle had a substance-exposed newborn (SEN) baby, exposed to meth. Danielle had previously enrolled in and successfully completed TERROS, the drug program the year before, when she had her first SEN baby, which died right after birth. The next baby, born a year later, had severe complications.

We held a team decision meeting (TDM); this was a serious situation. I believe the case was being treated as high profile because her first baby had died before, a year later, another SEN baby arrived. Everyone asked Danielle how she could have risked using drugs during her pregnancy, considering what happened to the first baby. My boss at the TDM said he could understand a relapse in general, but knowing she was pregnant and knowing about the inherent risks firsthand, he couldn't understand it. I agreed with my boss.

However, we gave her a few points because she had successfully completed TERROS once. (Most referred mothers do not bother to attempt to go through with the program. Most of them have the attitude that they love their children and would do anything for them except give up their drugs and/or complete a drug program. And they probably do love those kids, in their own deluded way. But old habits die hard.) In any case, while Danielle had finished the program, what was her success rate? She had another SEN baby a year later.

Looking at both sides, we strive to take the least restrictive course of action, so we filed an in-home dependency. My boss told me before the TDM that we would have to, because the case was high profile. I never knew the political aspects unless I was specifically informed of them. Because Danielle had originally delegated her mother-in-law as the safety monitor, it was agreed that Danielle would live with the mother-in-law and the baby and her other two kids.

We always speak of strengths in CPS, and one of Danielle's strengths was that the two older kids, ages four and six, had not been SEN babies. They were in school, had no special needs, and did very well at school. They seemed well adjusted and were very healthy. So that was taken into consideration in the scheme of things.

Often we run into ignorant mothers who have their parental rights terminated; they have another baby, thinking that at least they will have another child to hold on to. What those moms do not realize, of course, is that termination of parental rights is automatic cause for removal for any other child born, until the mother can go through the court system and prove that she is currently fit to parent. The process starts all over., Sadly, usually nothing changes.

Danielle's mother-in-law, Hildaga, did not speak English. This must have been during a time when we allowed illegal immigrants to be safety monitors, which our department no longer allows. This woman was an old-fashioned Hispanic woman, loving and maternal. She was devoted to her immediate family and to Danielle and Danielle's kids. She could set an example for the whole world; she did not judge Danielle but felt compassion. She wanted Danielle to straighten out. She did not want the kids taken from their mom if possible, and she was willing to sacrifice and serve as the 24-7 safety monitor in order to give Danielle a second, and probably, last chance. I was very impressed with Hildaga's character. She was modest, had a clean and loving heart, yet seemed to understand the ramifications involved.

Danielle was understandably scared as events unfolded. I told her to just keep her faith. Danielle said she knew she could "stay straight forever" at Hildaga's house. I figured this could be true but warned her not to abuse the privilege either. This woman was giving her a second chance, and Danielle needed to recognize that and stay focused on that second chance and not mess up anymore.

Once when I went to visit her, Danielle gave me a strange but nice compliment: "You make me feel happy when I see you." She said I relaxed her. I was not quite sure what she meant. But I tried to lighten the mood when feasible, I admit that. I also tried to show encouragement with a smile from time to time. I did not want her to stay focused on her anxiety but on her rightful actions, the actions that could actually help put those anxieties to rest if Danielle would do right and continue to do so. It was not above me to throw in bits of silly humor with Danielle sometimes, and I tried to reassure her things would be okay if she could stay on the straight and narrow.

Danielle told me that she had had a wonderful upbringing in a nice, middle-class family until one day when she and her parents were out in public. Apparently Danielle was an only child. The family stopped someplace, and, that fast, a drive-by shooting took place right there. Tragically, Danielle's mother was killed on the spot. It reminded me of Michelle, my sister's classmate. That is a very hard thing to deal with.

Everything took a downward turn after that. Danielle turned to drugs to numb the pain. This was after her dad, heartbroken, hooked up with a woman who became Danielle's stepmother. This woman, the stepmom, was the one who got Danielle hooked on drugs. Oh gosh, what a mess!

After that, Danielle hung with the wrong crowds, and the rest was the history of her meth usage. I contacted TERROS and had them update the info in their system so that when they worked with this mom, they could address the problem twofold: providing grief counseling and addressing the relapse factor specific to Danielle's individual situation. I reminded them of the fact that she had completed the TERROS program in its entirety the first time around before relapsing. Maybe they could suggest techniques when they understood her particular patterns of usage and the triggers that presented their unique challenges and hopefully help her succeed this time.

Danielle's little girl in kindergarten was bright and loved school. She alternated between spending time with Mom and her paternal grandmother: another grandmother, not Hildaga. Everyone lavished attention on her. The little toddler boy, Elijah, was cute too. He had longish curly black hair, with the longest eyelashes imaginable. When I first met him, I flirted with him, and he sucked it in. He smiled and turned around but suddenly started crying. I was concerned that I had upset him in some way.

"Oh no," Danielle replied. "This is a cultural thing in my family. Little boys do that when they like an outsider. They smile and then cry." I felt very flattered, if she was telling me the truth, that is.

I was happy that Hildaga had done what she did to help preserve this lovely family. Hildaga symbolized the mother Danielle had lost, as far as I was concerned. This was a perfect example of family-based practice, where everyone could win with effort, consistency, and working together.

And, to my knowledge, they did.

26

The Messina Case, the Phoenix PD, Workload, and Demographics

I was ready to finally take a vacation in July 2007. I had worked for CPS a year and a half by then and had only taken off a day here or a day there while working mega hours. The opportunity finally presented itself, thankfully. I guess you could say it was a divine intervention for me. I could have wound up ten feet under instead, for all I knew. Nobody but those working for CPS can even begin to fathom the large amount of work and stress the job entails. Phones ring off the hook. Service providers, sources, frantic parents or relatives, law enforcement, attorneys, and so on, call constantly, with explosions (emergencies) left, right, and in between. We never knew where or when a day would start or end.

The job is like beat the clock, but time is never on your side. Even closed cases can turn into major catastrophes down the line or at the whim of a bad moment. Then you are still stuck dealing with the aftermath. When I was younger, there was that series of horror movies: *Friday the Thirteenth*, I think. Jason kept coming back to life after they thought they had gotten rid of him once and for all. That was the kind of feeling you can get with this job. You finally "kill the monster," and all is well. Then one, or maybe six, years later, the same monster returns with more serious problems! Trust me, that happened so many times I lost count.

To give you an idea of the workload aspect I am talking about, let's say, for example, you go out on an investigation. There could be lots of kids, and the investigation could last for hours. Say the situation is very dire. Now you have to remove the children. That might take infinite hours to achieve. You might have to call your office for backup, if there is any available. You have to bring the kids to your office and fill out a bunch of placement packets and call the district office to request placement for the kids.

About a year or so ago, it got so bad that the district office ran out of placements. We had to keep whatever kids we'd removed at our desks for the entire day. After seven that night, we'd take them to the Phoenix night office (AHIT), and then pick the kids up again in the morning. This went on day after day until they could find a placement for the children. It was a nightmare, to put it mildly. Thankfully, it usually only took a day or a few days to place infants and toddlers. While we had the kids, we would have to feed them, change them, watch them, and so on. And do your job? Right. The temporary solution was opening up a resource center for the toddlers and babies and having babysitters at the resource center until the kids were placed in foster homes. We still might have to keep the older kids at our desks for a number of days until a group home opened up.

Even when I first started CPS, when they had enough placements, more often than not the district office was unable to place all the kids together. It's like calling hotels during the busy season. One might only have a room for one; another might have maybe two spots if you're lucky. It could take the district office a long time to get back to us. In the meantime, you have to pay attention to the kids! Some of them might be young troublemakers trying to get into everything. Some might be totally traumatized and need words of reassurance.

I once volunteered to watch a teen girl for a number of hours until I could take her to the AHIT office because they couldn't find her a group home or foster home. While I went to use the restroom for a minute, apparently she went around the office and stole a bunch of stuff from people's desks. It didn't come out until the next day. I felt thankful she didn't take my credit cards and run for the hills, using them along the way. By the time I would have found out, she could have racked up quite a bill.

When you hear back from district office, you might have to place one kid in Queen Creek, an hour in one direction, then the other in Sun City or Surprise, another hour and a half of driving. You might also have to stop in between to buy the kiddos dinner if you have had them for hours and you are going to be delivering them at ten at night, for example, or to a foster group home where the kitchen closes at seven.

If you are unlucky to have to go to court in the morning on another case and have a full schedule for the next few days, you might have to go back to the office and submit the Rapid Response forms for all those kids the same night, as well as the dependency worksheet, which is about twelve to thirteen pages. In addition, you have to enter the info in the system about where they have been placed, do your legal screens to show they have been removed, and so on.

Speaking of court, a case manager is required to complete all kinds of court reports. That takes a lot of time, especially in the first year, when you're not used to doing them.

When I first started with CPS, we were required to do the kinship home studies in connection with the court reports; we'd visit the relative placements and gather a bunch of information to assess if they would be a good placement. These days, CPS in Arizona employs outside agencies to do the home studies. (Note: the author currently works for such an agency, which licenses foster homes and conducts home studies.) We'd have to run background checks on anyone older than eighteen who lived in the home and also for relative placements. If there are a number of dads involved, which is more often than not, that all takes extra time. Also, a lengthy child-safety assessment has to be completed for each child.

Can you imagine how burdensome that can be when you are dealing with maybe five or ten kids in one family?

While some case workers do not take detailed case notes, we are supposed to. It could be an issue if we don't finish the case notes in a timely manner and something worse happens on the case. But it's quite a challenge to even find the time to do all the case notes along with all the other necessary reports. Let us not forget about having to pull prior CPS and police reports and review them. Actually, workers are supposed to do that before going out on the investigation. I had one case with thirty priors. That took time to review. But remember, we are supposed to meet our response time!

Maybe four to six reports per week does not sound like much, but what if some or all of them also involve two or more households (shared custody plus the significant other's children)? If the children attend various schools, it is generally policy that we visit the children at their individual schools. Have I mentioned the part of CPS policy that requires that the first time we visit a home, we have to go unannounced? There is a good chance nobody will be home. Even the people who call you back might not be there until you have gone twice and left two cards instead of just returning the call the first time. Some of them wait until the third time or make you track them down, literally. Some of the parents work late or many hours, so you might visit them at crazy hours or on weekends. If you cannot find the parents or kids, you have to go through channels to try to locate them.

Sometimes with removals, the kids might be placed at a distance. Maybe transportation for the parents' visits could not be arranged or falls through. If this happens and you are lucky, you might be able to ask a case aide to assist with the visit, but don't count on it if it is last minute. All case aides, as well as parent aides, require referrals. It could take from one to four weeks, depending on how backed up the services are. Case aides are usually not available for emergencies. If there is no case aide available for a visit between the parent/s and kids, guess who has to temporarily cover that visit?

Naturally, you do! Any doctor, whether psychological, psychiatric, and so on, generally requires case managers to be present for that first appointment for the child since they are the legal guardian; the professional needs information from them. That could easily take one or two hours. If the children are returned home, generally case workers have to transport them home, depending on their ages.

There are various meetings to attend, in addition to court: team decision-making meetings for proposed removals, returns, disruptions, age of majority, and so on. There are child/family team meetings (CFTs), generally one per child per month if the child receives services such as therapy. Sometimes a special staffing is needed when the case is not going well and the providers want to staff the case with case managers or when the attorney wants to staff the case, as well as regular staffing that must take place with supervisors. Speaking of providers: every time something does go wrong, do expect a phone call on a case, whether it is a removed child or not. At that point the case worker usually has to jump in there and do something about the situation. Guess what that means? You got it: more work.

A dependency case will be transferred to the ongoing unit after a while, but first you have to order the birth certificate, school and medical records, and so on. Again, imagine the volume of work if that involves a lot of kids in a given case. You have to prepare a very detailed case transfer summary, explaining all doctor visits, appointments, and so on. If a relative or parent lives out of state, you have to prepare what is called an ICPC (interstate compact on the placement of children) in case the child might be sent out of state. That is a lot of work. Thank goodness, there usually are secretaries to help with that type of paperwork. (Thanks, Terry!)

So there I was, a divorced, middle-aged woman with a child in the upper level of high school. I received minimal child support. There was no rich ex or anyone else to assist me (though some people didn't think twice about periodically criticizing and critiquing every little thing I didn't do right, just to add to the pile of stress).

Happily, I had a pretty nice child, with decent values and behavior. However, my child wanted but did not receive enough time or energy from me, unfairly. In my spare time, I ran around: grocery shopping, cleaning, cooking, taking the car for maintenance work, taking my son and I to dental and doctor appointments, to open houses at school, and fitting in a little fun time on the weekend for my son to go to his favorite places. All this while I was working fifty-five hours a week.

Maybe I am praising myself too highly, but I think it's safe to assume that the average person would have lost it under those circumstances,

I had recently lost my house and had to move while my son was on vacation. The move was astronomically difficult. I wound up hiring someone to help me who probably ripped me off. I was too busy to notice. I started dating an eccentric, difficult investor who wanted me to drive almost an hour each way to Mesa and back to meet him close to where he lived; I was still living in the west valley. It was probably a blessing in disguise that we only met once a week. Who had time? He could not understand why I eventually broke it off. I needed someone who could really be there for me, not just for a date. I never did find someone to fit the bill, but at least I managed to be there for myself. And God was always there for me, keeping me strong.

That was all that was happening while my mind was preparing for a vacation. Gina and Jorgio's case appeared to be a standard SEN case. The baby and Mom tested positive for meth. At first, the case seemed simple enough. The next-door neighbor, Lydia, was willing to be a safety monitor. Lydia was a conservative woman with no CPS priors and no criminal history. She felt sympathy for Gina, so she was willing to do it.

The Family Preservation service went to help Mom, find out what was going on, and offer suggestions and guidance for straightening out the home environment. The baby would stay at

Lydia's house, and Gina would go next door to visit the baby when she got off work or when Family Preservation was present.

Everything was basically fine until I received notification by email from Family Preservation voicing concerns about Gina and Jorgio's other two children, who'd be returning from Mexico "soon." I remember blinking stupidly. "Their other two children?" What was the deal with that? They had mentioned it to me in conversation once, but it did not register until the present moment.

My mind was at half-mast. I dug through the prior reports. Boy, what an ugly sensation that gave me! The two prior reports were about sexual abuse with the little girl, Misteria. "Oh, great!" I moaned. Vacation began in two days, but this was high on my scale. Immediate intervention or resolution was needed. All I needed was to leave and have something horrible happen and have to return in the harsh limelight. (Ask any CPS worker; their worst fear is to have a high-profile case where everyone is looking for the worker on the case. We prefer to stay anonymous, even those of us who have big mouths and are not afraid to use them.) Usually if people ask, "Where do you work?" my coworkers and I tend to say, "For the state of Arizona" instead of for CPS.

I collected my interpreter, Blanca, and we ran out to their apartment ASAP. We knew they would be home from work. I didn't beat around the bush, which I sometimes did, hoping the lies would reveal the answers better than the truth would. But my patience and my nerves were already at rock bottom. "What the heck was this all about?" I exclaimed, indicating the report with the sexual abuse allegations. Unfortunately, I could not gather any conclusions based upon the prior case notes or the police reports. As a matter of fact, I wound up getting into hot water with the Phoenix PD over it.

It started out innocently enough. I tried to contact the police detective working the case. When there is sexual or physical abuse, there is always police involvement. The detective assigned to the case was on vacation and would not be back until after I was on my vacation. I thought I came up with a brainstorm idea. I decided

I would send an email requesting the Phoenix Police department's "expertise opinion of the outcome of the case." Apparently the email went to everyone in the Phoenix PD. (So what? Don't they ever do "first come, first served"? Guess not.) Their interpretation was that my email implied that they hadn't done their job properly!

So my big boss (APM) arrived, telling me to lay low, saying that the whole Phoenix PD was mad at me. Also, he said to watch my emails from now on. And what raced through my mind? *The Phoenix PD has my name and can look up my DMV information. They have my license plate. They can have it in for me and make my life hell if they choose to.* Boy, I was in paranoid mode, let me tell you!

Thankfully, the Phoenix PD was way too busy with other more important issues. Also, they are not evil and they quickly forgot about me. Whew and hooray. Upon my return from vacation three weeks later, the first words out of my mouth to Anthony, our boss, was, "Are the police still after me?" He gave me great news. "No, they have other stuff to keep them busy, and you would be smart to not draw any further attention to yourself. You never know what they will do with you." Family Preservation asked me to contact the detective again on the case, and I told the team, "No. You can contact them if you want. Phoenix PD is still mad at me." They probably thought I was just being my flaky self. Self-preservation describes it better.

Back to the situation and case. Jorgio took and passed a lie detector test. I saw that noted in the police report. But Family Preservation expressed the strong possibility that he was "pawning off" Misteria in exchange for his drugs. I just about flipped out! "No!" I moaned, trying not to totally freak out. When I went over there with Blanca the night before, the parents appeared docile when I brought up the priors. I was wondering if that was a sign of innocence at first but then wondered if it indicated denial, minimizing, covering up—guilt, in other words.

To make a long story short, I removed the three kids and placed them at the paternal great-aunt's house. The paternal family loved

Gina and said they wouldn't mind if she came with the kids. They knew for fact that Jorgio was the bad influence. But Gina had been with Jorgio so long that she couldn't stand to be parted from him. Gina was still making poor decisions.

Jorgio, on the other hand, had warrants for domestic violence. He was supposed to take a DV (domestic violence) class to fulfill his obligations. I called and arranged it with his probation officer. However, that, too, backfired. Jorgio showed up a day late for class and was arrested for not appearing when he was supposed to. Since Gina and Jorgio were illegal immigrants, immigration wound up deporting Jorgio back to Mexico. By then, I had the case transferred to ongoing. For some reason, Gina and Jorgio's case reminded me of a CPS version of the movie *Good Fellas*: another chaotic story where nothing goes smooth from beginning to end, which actually describes a typical CPS case.

While I worked at the Glendale office covering Maryvale, the demographics revealed that the vast majority of my cases appeared to be illegal immigrants from Mexico. Quite a few of them partook in drug usage, especially meth. The majority of my cases, Hispanic and otherwise, involved single parents. (There is something righteous to be said for the sanctity of marriage when you look at those statistics. Maybe part of it is linked to the enormous stress of not having a committed partner to help with the kids.) Most CPS cases I worked involved bigger families; most of the families included a number of dads, sometimes as many dads as there were children. (And parents wonder why their kids are so mixed up and angry, having trouble functioning?)

Most of my cases involved parents with poor educations. A good number of them didn't work; if they did, they had menial jobs. A great number of the parents were either meth users or abusers of alcohol. Sex abuse, physical abuse, and neglect were prevalent. Those dynamics would change when I moved to the more middle-class Thunderbird office, where there were more out-of-control teenagers. In Maryvale, the majority of households were what we called "dirty houses," usually filthy. A good number of the kids were underfed and did not seem to receive good medical care, even when the parents received free medical coverage from AHCCCS (state insurance) and food stamps. I heard that hard-core meth users would trade food stamps for meth at a fraction of their value, and I believe it. That was probably true at all the CPS offices. Probably most other demographic factors were similar at other offices as well.

27

Della Mendez

Della Mendez had six kids. The CPS report was called in by the maternal grandmother, Alexa, when Della disappeared for two days, leaving the children, ages two through ten, unattended, without food, in a sleazy motel off I-17, somewhere around Indian School. The place was definitely acknowledged as a drug motel. I had gone there previously to help a coworker remove some toddlers while their mom was busy getting high, mething it up.

The eldest child was smart enough to call the paternal grandmother of the three youngest, who lived locally, and advise Barbara of their predicament. Though the girl did not know exactly where they were, the girl read the phone number to Barbara and told Barbara the room number they were in. Then Barbara called the motel, asked for the address, and arranged for the kids to be transported to her house. The maternal Grandma, Alexa, called in the CPS report and came and got the three older grandkids. Alexa lived somewhere near Flagstaff.

Mom had left the room at two in the morning. The kids did not hear from Mom at all. The eldest called Barbara twenty-four hours later. Both of the grandmas were willing to take the kids, and I was thankful that I did not have to file a dependency and take them into my custody. I got the report after the kids were safe with Grandma, so I did not have to serve a temporary custody notice

(TCN). Nonetheless, I still had to conduct the investigation, as I was the person the case was assigned to. It was thought at the time that something might have happened to Mom. I suggested that the two grandmas could perhaps check with the police, which they had not done. I felt bad for the kids. They all stated that Mom left them with no food. They also stated that Mom often went off with her friends and paid them little attention.

I was fuming. When I got back to my office, I received a call from Barbara that she'd called the police, and Della had been arrested in Scottsdale. She was then taken to Phoenix for a traffic warrant. The police were holding Mom at the Estrella jail, located on Durango, right near one of the Phoenix juvenile courts. I went to pay Mom a visit.

The first time I went to visit Della, they had her in a holding cell, so I couldn't see her at that time. I asked the correctional officer to take the safety monitor plan to her, which she signed and the officer returned to me. I forget how long Della was in jail for on her warrant, but I felt she should have been locked up and given extra time for deserting all her children in the middle of the night, without even leaving them food or supplies. In the back of my mind I also wondered whether when she was busted two days later she was even on her way back to her kids?

The maternal grandma said that Della had lived up on the Indian Reservation for a year and a half without having to pay rent. Della collected a minimum of $2,000 a month between social security, child support, and special funds for Native Americans. She had also stayed rent free at Barbara's when she returned to Phoenix for a number of months. Yet, naturally, Mom claimed she was broke when I met with her.

I did not think the conclusion farfetched that anyone who hasn't paid rent for two years but takes in $2,000 month, leaves a bunch of little kids at two in the morning, and is always broke must be doing hard drugs, especially if she is barely feeding the children. It was sad how a few of the kids even tried to cover for her. When I first asked Conrad, he said, "Mommy always feeds us." When I asked if he had food at the motel before they were picked up, he said, "No."

The children all had lice when they were first picked up by Barbara. If that wasn't enough, the three youngest also had ringworm. The oldest, Ellen, had had a rotten tooth for some time. I was infuriated! I wanted the police to officially charge Della with child abuse, and I told the detective working the case that. She said they could charge her with a misdemeanor, but a felony charge was harder to convict on.

Della contacted a male friend to pick up the check from social security to bail her out. I instructed Barbara to not comply; that was not what the check was for. It was money for the kids, not Mom's bail money. I also called and warned Mom's friend not to come get the money. Later, when I interviewed Della, she indicated she planned to pay the money back, and I indicated I did not necessarily believe that.

Della was finally released from jail, but she never showed up for the TDM. We found out she was staying a few days at a Day's Inn or Motel 6 in Mesa. I called and left her a message about the TDM. Conveniently, she called Barbara right after the TDM was over and claimed she did not get the message. I was starting to like Della less and less.

One thing was for sure: I did not want Della to be alone with the kids. Nor did I trust her with them. I did not have much recourse. It was Barbara's decision to allow Della to stay with her and the three little ones. I personally felt that Barbara was too intimidated to tell Della no. Barbara had lost her son, Guy, the father of the three little ones, in a car accident. Though Guy and Della had never married, they were together as a couple when Guy was killed. I would wager that Della played off her mother-in-law's emotions. In any case, I provided family services, including Family Preservation and free child care, since Barbara worked. I signed Della up to do a drug program and drug testing.

I was more shocked than anyone when Della finished TERROS

(the name of the drug testing program) successfully. It was stated at the TDM that Della had done drugs a long time, and I believed that. At the interview, she had adamantly refused to do a drug program, but in the long run she wasn't given a choice. I was still trying to second-guess Della. She had to stay off drugs or risk losing that $2,000 a month. So Della had a great motivator. But what about when it was all over? The grandmothers were always there, and I mentioned guardianship, if needed. Most Native American do not prefer severance of parental rights.

I was subpoenaed to go to court more than six months later because the police detective had decided to charge Mom with a felony. The case was dismissed because neither of the grandmothers appeared. The police detective was pleased when I told her I had substantiated child abuse against Mom in my report findings. That was the least I could do. But then the detective said my boss at Glendale said otherwise. So I explained that in the report findings, I'd had to keep rewording it until finally the substantiation review team was willing to accept the proposed substantiation in the proper format. With CPS, there is always so much red tape, from the beginning right up to the gory end.

28

Christine Hannory

Christine might have very well been the first and perhaps only child I felt little sympathy and liking for. I felt she was a cunning and manipulative fourteen-year-old girl who was into all the wrong things. Was it her parents' fault? That is hard to say. Her siblings were all well behaved and appropriate. They went to a religious grade school, with the exception of her older brother, who went to a public charter high school. The kids all did well in school.

Christine had dropped out. Christine was a pretty girl and too smart for her own good. If she was not careful, she would wind up being sold as a part of a sex trafficking ring. She liked drugs too much, which was why I believed that could happen to her.

The report was made by one of our associate agencies, which Christine was receiving counseling from. Christine had told her therapist, Eileen (Christine's mom was also named Eileen, so it was easy for me to remember their names, though usually I am horrible with names), that she was afraid to go home, that her older brother had beat her. She showed the counselor a few marks. The report also stated that Christine was into drugs. Christine had run away from home for three months. It was mentioned that Christine had taken up with older guys, possibly for the purpose of prostitution to supply her drug habits. Christine hemmed and hawed around that issue but admitted she'd stayed at an older guy's house for a while.

Eileen, Christine's mom, constantly came and went. Eileen and Haog, the dad, were never married. They had four children. Eileen had a boyfriend she would go to the house with when the dad was at work. I had a horrible first impression of Eileen upon meeting with her. But my opinion started changing. For example, Mom went to the house when the kids came home from school to tend to them and then left when Dad got home. So I relaxed my poor impression of her.

Haog, the dad, was from Vietnam, and he did not speak any English. He worked hard all day to support his family. I felt very sorry for him and felt his intentions were honorable. He was a foreigner who did not speak English but was a respectful person; he was just trying to do the best to support his family. Eileen was very soft spoken, a person who had special needs but who tried to do right by her kids the best she could. Eileen loved all the kids a lot, and they were all close to her, including Christine. My distinct impression was that Christine knew how to play her mother to perfection.

Christine maximized what she could get out of Mom in a way that would benefit or suit her the most. We sent Christine to a group home, where Christine was nothing but trouble. She was defiant and immediately picked a fight. I found out at the TDM that she was well versed at lying through her teeth. Eileen, the therapist, was on a conference call and stated that Christine had told the therapist her mom would always ask the children for money. Christine would not agree to the statement or argue it. She merely rolled her eyes upward, as if to convey that she had no idea what Eileen, the therapist, was talking about.

After the TDM, Eileen, the mom, was in tears over that comment and said to Christine, "How could you have let Eileen say those things about me. You know they're not true." Again, Christine remained silent. It seemed an admission of Christine's guilt to me; I was standing there and witnessed it firsthand. Because of Christine's and Eileen's actions, I realized that Christine was playing both the therapist and Mom.

Christine constantly called her mom and demanded that Eileen do something for her, and Eileen always would, because she loved her child and/or because she was afraid of losing her. Christine's siblings all claimed Christine was trouble, from the six-year-old up to the seventeen-year-old. The younger ones said they loved Christine but that she beat on them and hurt them. They seemed happy now that she was out of the house. The older brother said that if he hurt his sister, it was because she was so out of control he did not know what else to do. His dad was still working, and at the time his mom was not there. He looked at me with such soulful, sad, and beseeching eyes that I felt for him and the position he was put in.

There was a another issue with the ongoing case manager the case was transferred to. Abruptly, Laurie was fired. I had just transferred from the Glendale office to the Thunderbird office. The rumor I heard was that Laurie was doing stuff that violated policy, stuff the rest of us would never think of doing. She started bringing her own children to court. Sometimes she took kids who were supposed to be in foster care to her own home so her children could play with the foster kids. Before Laurie was fired, she had mentioned that Christine had run away from the group home and that she was going to be placed at Vision Quest. I heard it was located somewhere around Tucson, in the middle of nowhere.

Even that did not work out for Christine. Last I heard, Christine was AWOL and probably up to her old shenanigans, doing drugs, maybe involved in prostitution. She was probably focused on whom she should use next to achieve her goals. Hopefully it wasn't her family members. They had already suffered enough because of her as it was.

29

Eva Montanegro

Jacqueline had an SEN baby. The drug both Eva and the baby tested positive for was meth, of course. Eva was a strung-out sort of girl, staying with her boyfriend at her maternal grandma's house. Grandma told me flat out that she was too old to be a safety monitor. I wasn't worried about it. When the baby was born, it weighed less than two pounds. If it lived, it would not be going home from the hospital for some time.

I could not believe the size of the baby when I saw it in the baby ICU ward. She obviously had no meat on her. She was hooked to tubes and a ventilator. She was the length of a hand and half as wide, the poor little thing.

Eva's mother, Susan, came every day to see the baby. She seemed an upbeat, no nonsense, caring and efficient type of person. I felt she was more than appropriate as a safety monitor. Miraculously, the child was going to make it; she was scheduled for a release date. I went to Susan's house to check it out. It was a spotless house, beautiful, in a decent neighborhood. I had every intention of making Susan the safety monitor. Susan was discussing the idea of letting Eva live with her until Eva could be trusted on her own.

We had a TDM before the baby's release from the hospital. I had done a background check on the grandma. She told me that she had messed up eighteen years earlier. The charges appeared mostly about marijuana, but there was also one cocaine charge. Because she had been caught several times with drugs, Susan was given a year jail sentence. In Susan's own words, it more or less cost her everything, including her marriage. As she sat in jail, she wondered what she had done to her life. She had several small children at home that now did not have a mother to watch them.

Upon Susan's release, she vowed to stay away from drugs and never look back. Susan remarried and worked part-time, cleaning a few doctors' houses. She had finished dental school and had worked in the dental field. Susan was able to provide requested letters of reference. The doctors had praised Susan for doing an outstanding job, said that she was trustworthy, diligent, and reliable. I called one to ask whether Susan would be suitable for keeping the baby, and he thought absolutely yes, due to her reliability.

We needed a TDM, but my supervisor was out that day, as well as our usual TDM person. The replacement TDM supervisor and I remained friends until she was fired (another typical CPS story), but she had a reputation for filing dependencies on all her cases. Since Susan had an old drug history, I was told that we should just file the dependency and let the court decide. I thought that was totally unnecessary, plus a waste of taxpayer's money.

The next day I had a brainstorm. Susan had called me with the information about Eva's adult sibling, who had a clean background, to see if the adult sibling could take the baby. I ran the background check, and it was fine. I also checked the sibling's boyfriend, since she lived with her boyfriend. Cassandra and Eva, the mom, were definitely opposites. Cassandra was so down on drugs that she would not even allow Eva to know where she lived. If Eva wanted to see the baby, Cassandra agreed to bring the baby to Susan's house for the visit. Cassandra was expecting at the time, but I felt it should be okay, since the boyfriend and extended family were willing to help out.

So I staffed it with my supervisor. She was willing to override the recommendations of the TDM. I am not sure if that was "legal," but my supervisor was new, and she was okay with my plan. She would have been the person making the decision at the TDM if she had not been out sick that day. I think we had mentioned Cassandra at the TDM, but they just poo-pooed the idea; Cassandra was only nineteen and expecting herself. So what? If the person passed a background check, who were we to say the person wasn't responsible enough to serve as the placement if she wanted to? She had enough income to watch the child. That was the main thing—that and passing the background check. My supervisor only requested I go check out the home, which I would have done anyway.

Cassandra lived on the far side of Mesa, closer to Queen Creek. But it was a clean and new area. The neighborhood was appropriate and safe.

Eva did not like the idea of the baby being with her sister. I told Eva that at least the baby was not with a stranger, and she changed her attitude immediately and thanked me. I told Eva the best way to get her baby back was to do all the necessary services: drug testing, TERROS drug program, and Family Preservation. Naturally, Eva didn't do any of it.

Fast forward: I got a call from the Mesa Police one day. They said they were at Cassandra's house and that I needed to come and intervene; it concerned the baby. At first I was I was alarmed that something had gone haywire with Cassandra watching the child. When I got there, Cassandra and Susan were arguing. Susan said the thirty days of the safety monitor plan were over and that she wanted to take the baby. Susan had every intention of filing for guardianship of little Dory.

Cassandra was very attached to Dory and was fearful that if Susan took Dory, Eva would have easy access to her. I gently reminded Cassandra that if it had been a dependency, the mother was still granted privileges to see her child, usually twice a week. Cassandra retorted, "But Eva isn't doing services!" Many parents don't, I wanted to tell her, but still they had rights to see their kids until their rights were severed.

The cops sat there, waiting for me to make a decision. It had taken me an hour to get there, so I think it is safe to say they were running out of patience. Their attitude was probably "We don't care what you do, just hurry" by that time, and I can't say I blame them for that.

I was reviewing whether Susan was financially stable. She had been living in her house a long time with her husband. They owned the house. Her husband worked a steady job. Truthfully, Susan was better equipped to handle the child.

On the other hand, I was thinking of the TDM and not wanting to violate policy. I finally commented that we should call Susan's ex-husband, Cassandra and Eva's dad, the maternal grandfather, and see if he would be willing to be the safety monitor, since he had a clean background check. He was not far away and said he would come right over. The police begged me to leave, if I felt I had the situation under control. I told them yes and thanked them for their help. Cassandra was willing to go along with her dad's decision. She loved him dearly and was always close to him, especially during those bad years.

When Mr. Montanegro arrived, he conferred privately with me. He advised me that he and Susan still spoke on a semiregular basis. He could vouch that Susan never went back to drugs and that she was a more appropriate caregiver than Cassandra, considering the circumstances. Also, Mr. Montanegro advised me that he lived very close to Susan and he would be happy to be the safety monitor. If we let Susan take Dory, he would guarantee me that he would check on the baby every day if need be, or whatever CPS required. The man was very distinguished and reputable, so I called my supervisor and explained the dilemma. She said it sounded solid but advised that I needed to broach the family again about filing guardianship if they wanted to avoid a dependency. So I did.

Mr. Montanegro then talked to Cassandra and told her she

must do what was best for the baby. With tears in her eyes, she told her dad she would. Mr. Montanegro said that Susan would take the child, so premature at birth, to all her many appointments, as there were a number of medical needs. Finally Cassandra relented and, crying, she handed the baby over. I felt very uncomfortable watching all this. Some people might think being in my situation and witnessing all these messy scenarios taking place is cool, but it's really not.

The family wasted no time in getting the guardianship filed. Later I heard that Cassandra and her boyfriend broke up. I was sad to hear that but also thought about how difficult it would have been for Cassandra to have two children to contend with as a single parent at her age. One child was enough for her to deal with.

I went to check on the baby about a month or so later. My supervisor suggested I do that and then close the case out. I was amazed at how much Dory had finally grown. She went from being a little tiny stick figure to a healthy-looking baby. She weighed nine pounds at three months old. She was doing excellent, according to her doctors.

Eva went to see the baby once, really high at the time, and almost dropped her child. Susan gave Eva hell and told her to leave and not come back until she could straighten her act out. All things considered, I felt good about how the case ended, not with Eva but with the extended family.

And that is what it means when CPS refers to family-centered practice, for the extended family can pick up the slack with the children even when the parents cannot do what is required, as long as they can ensure the safety of the child. Thank God for the extended family once again came through for this particular child. We turn to family-based strengths to mend the broken pieces.

PS No other CPS report needed to be filed on this child!

30

Tina Dorstum

I had one case where the mom called the police on her thirteen-year-old boy. They proceeded to lock him up at juvenile hall. I was to pick him up the next day. The mom, Tina, told me that her son and boyfriend had gotten into it. I believe she said the reason she came to the boyfriend's defense was because Billy, her son, had started the incident.

I got a much different version from Billy when I talked to him. Billy said he could not handle the domestic violence, drugs, and everything else going on. We held a TDM meeting, and Tina wound up cussing like a truck driver on a drunken binge. What set Mom off was us asking about Gary, her ex, Billy's dad. Her crude, foul language in front of her son did nothing to boost my confidence in Tina. She confessed to being bisexual, which also did not help matters. Tina never put Gary's name on the birth certificate. She claimed he was worthless and that was why she had dodged him. It didn't matter that Gary was professing love for the child or that he called Billy every night or that Billy loved his dad. It equally didn't matter that Gary came across as soft spoken and polite. Tina would have nothing to do with any of it. Poor Gary was happy to take a paternity test but did not have the money for it, and I advised him we could not pay for it. I had advocated that Gary should get it done, no matter how long he had to wait.

I scheduled an intake meeting with Billy and Jewish Family Services. I attended that meeting because I was required to. Jose asked Billy, "Have you ever done any drugs?" I don't know about Jose, but I nearly fell out of my chair when Billy replied that he had smoked grass with his mother before, a long time ago. It made me mad that Mom had smoked with her child. She did not deny it or appear embarrassed or admit her behavior was out of line.

I opted we do a ninety-day voluntary regarding Billy. I figured this would give his mom time to get her act together, which I personally doubted she would, based on the above. To compound matters, she told us she was now homeless, so that was another obstacle she had to work against. I became more frustrated when Tina began to miss her scheduled visits with Billy. She claimed her boyfriend had disappeared, but then she said he had taken the car one day, that they still shared it.

I was curious and left a business card at the room where Mom, Billy, and the boyfriend had stayed. Tina called me back and put the boyfriend on the phone. I didn't like that Tina had told Billy when they moved to Arizona that they were moving to get away from the boyfriend, but when they got here, the boyfriend was here, still in on everything. And Billy did not like the violence between his mom and her boyfriend. I can't say I blame him for that!

Tina never reformed, and the biological dad did not get Billy. Billy was shipped back to live with his stepdad in Ohio, where Billy and his mom had originally moved from.

31

The Baby Who Died

An SEN baby died. He was two pounds when he was born and had a lot of medical complications. He was so cute, a pretty little biracial boy with a perfectly formed head, handsome face, and beautiful eyes seeking hope. The mom, Trish, was separated from the boyfriend. They both came to see the baby at the hospital, but Dad was drunk when he showed up. The hospital staff told him he had to leave and could come back only if he were sober.

It was sad that there was domestic violence between the couple, so they had not had a very promising start. That was also the reason for their separation. I was glad to see that Trish was trying to act responsibly. She confided to me that she was very involved in her church. She had been in recovery (from drugs) for some time (or so she said), with the help of her church. She mentioned she prayed for her baby and knew he would be okay. I did not have the same confidence that he would live, though I truly wanted him to. Trish was staying at the grandma's house. If the baby had lived and come home, Grandma would be the delegated safety monitor. The grandma had a nice house and treated Trish well, because Mom was being appropriate and serious minded about everything.

Trish prayed hard for the child, of that I have no doubt. But the damage from her substance abuse while still pregnant took its ultimate toll on the infant.

The baby died one day after gallantly struggling to survive. Though I offered Trish services, she refused them. I told her I could provide her grief counseling and that I felt she needed it. She was very agitated, and I understood that. I hoped this chain of events would not lead her back into meth, but it seemed like maybe it would be all too easy for just that to happen, especially since she was unwilling to engage in grief counseling (but drugs can mask all pain, supposedly).

Previously Trish had a child by another man. That child lived with his dad, but Trish was at least able to visit with him every other weekend. I hoped that this other child would keep her motivated to live her life on a better path, if not presently, then somewhere soon down the line.

I remember seeing that little baby hooked up to the IV, struggling to survive, a look of shock or dismay on his face: "Why do I have to do so much work just to live?" He was busy contending with that while Trish, his mom, lived in meth la la land. And the wage on mindless meth continues, taking more innocent lives in its wake.

32

Victoria Lucas

Victoria had a scary CPS report. Not only was she doing meth, she was also threatening neighbors' lives. It stated that she had left her kids in the car for fifteen minutes during the hot, hot Arizona summer. That type of stuff was in the report. As luck would have it, when I went to see Victoria, her children were not there. The three little ones were at Grandma's house. Victoria was so methed out when I first met with her she was hardly coherent. She made sounds, but they were not words, to my knowledge. She kept playing with her hair. She reminded me of someone who had just been committed to a loony bin for life.

It got worse. Victoria said there was a conspiracy against her by her family, that someone was out to kill her as they had killed someone else (and she was the only one who knew about it, of course). I asked the name of the person who had been killed, but Victoria did not know his name. Victoria was tweaking so badly that her head kept jerking, as well as her hands. Severe meth is known to produce hallucinations and paranoia. Sure, that made sense. You put a bunch of harmful chemicals into your body, what do you expect to happen? It's not going to make you a productive clear thinker living a good life, that is for sure. (Then why do so many people succumb to it, destroying lives in the process?)

When I went to check on Victoria's kids at Grandma's house,

little did I know that Victoria would follow me over there and fly into the house, screaming and carrying on. Her poor one-year-old immediately broke down and cried over seeing her mother in such a state of disarray. I was anxious to get out of there. So horrid were Victoria's ranting and raving that I whispered in Grandma's ear to call the police if Victoria did not calm down or leave, so as not to endanger the children. I mentioned that Grandma should keep the door locked from then on.

I served Victoria the temporary custody notice (TCN) the next day. First I knocked at Victoria's door, but she did not answer. I left the notification in her mailbox. I was shocked that she did call me back once she had it in her possession. She was given the information as to the court date and time, and she acted very sane, considering what I had been witness to the night before. Victoria was required to have a psychological evaluation and engage in mental health counseling, as well as participate in the TERROS drug program and drop UAs, and so on.

When we held the TDM, naturally Victoria did not appear. I found out that Victoria collected around $2,000 per month between social security and other monies. Yet when Grandma watched the kiddos, which was a lot, Victoria never compensated her monetarily at all. And Victoria was staying in a tiny one-bedroom dump in a bad part of town. Furthermore, she was evicted for not paying rent. I think we can figure out where all the money was going: to drugs. I was really angry about it and asked Mercy Care, formerly known as Magellan, formerly known as Value Options (our mental health provider for AHCCCS, the state-qualified insurance), if they could get Mom's social security taken away since she was spending it all on drugs. The Magellan people at the TDM said they would note it, whatever that meant. I think I later notified Social Security, or they did. That gave Mom motivation to clean up: she needed her income.

The dad of one of the kids, Donald, was a nice guy. He wound up taking his daughter. He called me the night before court and said he was the dad. This was news to me, and I said so, but I gave him the court information as well. I knew that the court would automatically order a paternity test if there was any question. I told Donald if he had any paperwork stating paternity that it would be ideal to bring it to court, which he did. Donald told me at court that Victoria had called him frantically when she received the TCN, and that was how he found out about the whole situation.

Before I released the child to him, I went to his house. Donald had a nice family: a dad and sibling. They were peaceful, sweet people. The grandfather had been a pro football player for the Detroit Lions a number of years ago, so that was very interesting. I love football, so naturally we devoted a few minutes to talking about the game. The grandfather said you wouldn't believe how hard on the body the game really was, and I thought to myself, *Kind of like my job—only mine's hard on the mind.* They had a nice house but not lavish. They were modest, churchgoing folk. Grandfather had raised his own two children, which really impressed me. Victoria and her mom did not want the beautiful girl going to that family, but the placement was affirmed when the judge ordered it. I was secretly glad. Plus, Grandma had her hands, full so it was one less child for her to care for.

Victoria said that Donald was never there for his little girl, but Donald told a story of Victoria bringing the little girl around as long as Donald would give her money in exchange. He also paid child support. Donald said he would not keep the child from seeing her grandmother.

When the psych evaluation date came, Victoria was nowhere to be found. The other services got dropped. I was expecting it, because I saw how far gone she was when I first did the investigation. I was surprised it took her as long as it did to disappear.

Too many mothers fit that scenario. They say they will do anything to keep their kids, but the truth of the matter is they won't. Most of them will barely lift a finger for their children, which is why they wind up having their children removed in the first place. They're only fooling themselves. As far as verbalizing their commitment, most of it is meth hype, with no substance behind the words. When it pertains to drugs or a significant other, these women will not put their kids first, no matter what lip service they give, to the point where they sometimes don't even consider their kids or their kids' feelings at all. Like my Glendale boss used to say, "Welcome to CPS." (Where old habits die hard, and insight is the common denominator that divides more often than it reunifies.)

33

Adoptions: Tim Ferguson

The paperwork part of CPS is quite lengthy, to put it mildly. And it is definitely time consuming. I decided to switch units. I needed a break from investigations. If I thought investigations meant a lot of paperwork, guess what? There was, or seemed to be, even more paperwork involved in adoptions. Plus the head honchos, who made all our counterproductive decisions, changed the child-safety assessment. It went from a struggle to be user friendly to a long, scrolling document, from twenty or so pages to approximately an eighty-page document—per case, that is. If we were given four cases a week, it was almost like writing a short book a week. Luckily that did change quickly, and they shortened it again, but then they made other horrible changes that neutralized the good change.

In any case, in my naivety, I thought adoptions would be positive and upbeat for the children, that they would finally have resolution. That was my own illusion. I failed to realize it was still CPS. There are few happy endings in CPS. Private adoption is another story: yes, someone probably saw a lot of joy there! With CPS, maybe some endings are okay, maybe bearable or doable, but happy? That pushes the envelope.

What can I say? The truth is a hard pill to swallow.

CPS adoption is kind of the opposite scenario of private adoption, where nothing is planned out. Removal and trauma to children was involved. Some children experience severe behavioral and medical conditions. These kids, whatever age, do carry baggage, even the toddlers. Think of the earlier chapter about Dana Christian. She was only a baby when Dad sexually abused her; she was close to suicidal by the time she was a preteen. What went away once she was adopted? Not the reality of her past! See my point? Thank goodness, she settled into a foster home with a family who did love her. They adopted her and tried to do right by her. But that kind of adoption was totally different than a young mom having a baby and giving it up at birth to a good stable family from the onset.

Some of these kids live a life of shame, stigma, and guilt before adoption day comes. I admire and respect families and individuals willing to adopt and provide a helpless child with a nice, loving home. I pray the child will heal through their adoption and new life. But who knows? Some do, and some don't. Most probably don't.

I worked in adoptions long enough to see one case through to adoption day. The case had been in the adoption unit for two years, I think, but every time the family got a new case worker, the person would quit. I was no different, but I did stay long enough to get their particular case finalized, probably because they wouldn't stop complaining. Rightfully so, I must add.

The case involved the Fergusons. They seemed to be a nice couple. How sweet Tim was to adopt his cousin's kid. The cousin was all methed out and wanted nothing to do with the baby. Baby Elizabeth by then was one. Tim and Brenda were as appropriate a family as one could find, or so I thought.

After leaving adoptions, I found out that Tim had lost his own child ten years ago through CPS involvement due to his meth usage at that time. The coworker working the case told me she noticed it on the kinship home study. Did I somehow not see it among the zillion pages of paperwork? How did I overlook that? I was glad that Tim was no longer that old meth person he once had been, but no wonder they were having trouble getting the adoption home study done. Good luck, new adoption worker.

34

Darrell Menson

I thought adoptions would be joyous. With CPS, there was so much hardship, it minimized the joy. I had one client, Darrell Menson, and his adorable grandson, Drake. Drake was a cute sandy-blond tot, a year and a half old, with longish hair, a fetching, impish smile, and the charming antics only a tot that age is capable of. He wore little blue jeans, loved his cars, liked to open the patio door (and close it and open it—Grandpa stood by, telling him to watch out that he didn't shut the door on his tiny fingers).

Darrell and Drake lived in a beautiful area a couple miles from where I was living at the time. I lived on the cusp between Peoria and Glendale (Arrowhead, to be exact, the newer part of Glendale). We were sandwiched between—I should say next door to—Sun City. On the other side of Sun City was Surprise, Arizona. That part of Glendale, where the sports stadium, is a busy little area. On Bell Road were a lot of shops and restaurants, especially by my street, Eighty-Third Avenue.

Darrell's area, though maybe only two miles farther north, was like being out in the country. (I later moved east, by Apache Junction, which was also like being out in the country.) Anyway, Darrell's particular subdivision had large houses on large lots. That in itself was a bit of a rarity, at least here in Arizona. In many of the new communities, no matter how big the houses, the lots seemed

126

piled on top of each other (like my current development). Darrell's house was a little older than most of the houses on his block. He might have been "the first guy on the block."

In any case, Darrell had an exquisite backyard. I brought over the adoptions paperwork when I first received the case. We sat at Darrell's kitchen table to go over it. What a view I witnessed! I saw horses in his yard, and the sun was setting in the background, a vibrant hot-pinkish purple. *What a spectacle*, I thought. Darrell was a rather somber man, about fifty, hard-working, conservative, well-mannered, and respectful. He had recently lost his wife to cancer.

So Darrell was facing a double hardship: the wife he was married to for many years was suddenly gone, his beautiful but energetic grandson's no-good mother ran off when Drake was born to go do her meth. Darrell and his wife had adopted the mom, Cindy, when she was a baby. They raised her in a good home. One only wonders if something in Cindy's genes led her to the path of deprivation she was on, the same one Cindy's biological mom was on when Darrell and his wife had adopted Cindy as an infant.

But please don't get me wrong. I am not trying to make excuses for the unfit mother. I definitely believe in free will and that, yes, there is a God, and, yes, we have a choice to do either what is morally right or not. Nobody is perfect; that's understood. But at some point, on some level, hopefully every last one of us will do what is right, no matter how long it takes us to get there (especially concerning a child who is the helpless, innocent victim in any scenario).

If I haven't said this previously, let me add or repeat it now: if I seemed somewhat soft on some or most of my clients compared to most other CPS workers, more tolerant, more accepting, if I seemed more positive to them than I needed to be, than was necessary or desirable, it was only because I truly wanted to believe I could reach them on a "higher plane." I thought that maybe the kindness would breed understanding, or at least some insight, especially if their own upbringing had been severely lacking. Leopards don't change their spots, as the saying goes, but chameleons do take on the characteristics of their surroundings. Parents often hand down the same fate over and over. And we workers try to provide services to the parents to change those behaviors. Once in a rare while, a person changes. It may be rare, but at least the justice system, coupled with the social work system, allows that opportunity.

Anyway, I still sought to overcompensate, and I admit it. I tried to convey, especially to the less privileged, that if you can't offer your kids much in the way of physical comforts and material means, don't worry. Try at least to offer them plenty of love and encouragement and good values. I always, in one way or another, pled for that much. Also, I encouraged parents to find something for their children to be motivated by so they might succeed. If I was with a teen and he saw a car he liked, I would tell him to work hard so he could have a car just like that one day. My point to him and to all kids is that what they want is attainable in our physical lives if they just believe in themselves.

The last time I saw Darrell before I switched from adoptions, he'd heard that his daughter was somewhere in New Mexico, pregnant again. Luckily Drake had not been a SEN baby. Grandpa made sure that Mom didn't do drugs during her first pregnancy. She was living at home (their home) at the time. Mom had the baby while living with them, but she split after Drake was born. Maybe this new baby wouldn't be so lucky. Maybe he would be a SEN with medical problems. And then presumably Mom would desert him as well? Hopefully not.

It is sad. Drug moms reproduce a lot, sometimes leaving extended families to try to clean up the messes they have caused behind them. It doesn't matter to those who prefer to stay irresponsible if someone else has to handle it all and do all the work while the ones not held accountable go upon their merry ways. Sometimes this is the extent of our family-based practice when some family members are drug users and some are not, when some individuals choose to reform and some do not, or when some family members have unresolved or untreated mental health issues and do not seek proper treatment or resist treatment.

35

Jamison Wane and Looking for a Higher Consciousness

Jamison was a lovely boy, a great athlete. He looked kind of like a young Tom Brady, quarterback for the New England Patriots. We all know how great Brady is. Some of us hate him to death just for his superior talents and being in so many Super Bowls! Jamison had the biggest blue eyes; you could get lost in them. He was the oldest of his siblings. Jamison and his two siblings had seen far too much with their young eyes, including a murder. I don't know how old they were when they witnessed the murder, but Jamison and his sibling Roxanne had been in their present foster placement for two years. And they had been at several other placements before that, one lasting six months. At the time the case came to the adoptions unit, Jamison was about eleven and his sister maybe eight or nine. The third sibling, Larry, was only six and was with his paternal grandma. So you can just imagine how young and vulnerable these kids were when they witnessed the murder.

It wasn't just the murder they witnessed; plenty of domestic violence led up to it, according to the case notes. Mom had been a stripper who liked to use meth. This was not uncommon for strippers. Not all of them are hard-core drug users or alcoholics, just most of them. In addition, Jamison's mom had many boyfriends and had produced three kids with three different dads and was pregnant with child four. The man who was murdered, which the children witnessed, was a random drug dealer.

Mom had proven herself totally unworthy and incapable of caring for her kids. She had child number four after her parental rights had already been severed from the first three kids. Jamison, being the oldest child, was most affected by that. Then, as if all that wasn't enough, Jamison's dad waltzed nonchalantly back into his life, promising Jamison everything under the sun before he made his final disappearing act. Did people really actually wonder why this poor little boy was filled with such rage? I didn't wonder, and I am not even a therapist. I knew why. Just look at the history of him and his family! Life had dealt Jamison an ugly hand, and Jamison knew he didn't deserve it but didn't know how to change or rectify it. After all, Jamison was only a kid, a victim of circumstances.

Jamison raged. I tried to reassure the brokenhearted kid—what else was there to do? What can one even say to a kid in his predicament? I talked sports with him. He loved sports and excelled at them. Since Jamison reminded me of Tom Brady physically, and since I believe humor can be good medicine, I commented to Jamison about what a great athlete Tom Brady was, even if the SOB never smiled. This comment won a smile from Jamison. I knew Jamison admired Tom Brady. All I was hoping for was a smile to ease Jamison's pain. Nonetheless, I told Jamison my deepest feelings: that the world is full of order, even though Jamison had seen only chaos.

I felt like Jamison and I somehow shared a valuable secret, a secret of the universe, that everything is there for the taking if you can get it right in your brain. I talked to Jamison about a fascinating book I was reading, *The Power of the Subconscious Mind* The book talked about the forces of nature being neither good nor evil; it was all in the way we used them. The guy who wrote the book was a chemist turned priest who put it well: "Water can drown a person or quench one's thirst. Electricity can light our house or electrocute us." How we used the forces of nature determined our outcome.

Why did I tell this boy about that book? I wanted his rage to go elsewhere. I wanted to distract him. Hell, I'd waged my own battles with rage in the past, and I wasn't so sure if I had come up short every time myself. But I wished for Jamison some self-control, some future, some higher thoughts to turn to and ponder, even if he fell short of them. I felt if I could present Jamison with thoughts in an orderly but mystical way, that maybe he would buy into it despite the past. I loved visiting Jamison every month. He was special to me.

Jamison became defiant one day, and his adoptive parents spanked him. Spankings were prohibited by adoptive parents—and in any CPS foster placements, for that matter. My supervisor at the time said the licensing agency should have dealt with the issue, but apparently they had not. A CPS report was called in at the time I was making the transition from adoptions back to investigations.

Although most people in adoptions—and every other unit— believe that adoptions is a piece of cake, I beg to differ. I think it is harder, trickier, than the investigation stage, when you go to assess the situation, make a determination, provide services, and in some case recommend removals as a last resort. You pass the case on. No matter how overwhelmed with work you are, at least you can address the horrors in each case. In ongoing, you can still maintain hope; you have not arrived at the end of the road. Adoptions seemed to involve so much more than that because adoption is final, even when it isn't final. Adoptions was too definitive to me than other units, and not in a good way. I wanted what was less definitive, if definitive had to look that bad. Time and experience taught me that hard lesson while I was working with CPS.

Anyway, while I was getting back into the groove of investigations, I received a call from Jamison's adoptive mom on a Sunday evening on my work cell phone. She said that Jamison had punched the other little foster girl (not his sister Roxanne but another kid) hard, in the stomach. He'd then grabbed a knife and held it against his chest while screaming. Finally Jamison flung the knife away and went up to his room.

Candy was beside herself and didn't know what to do. She asked if I could come out there. I told her I would, even though I was exhausted. I suggested that she call a CPS report in to the hotline and explain that Jamison was out of control. Candy asked about calling the Impact Crisis team as an alternative; I did think that was a better alternative, especially since they had already worked with the family while in crisis. This was not a first-time referral; they had been out there a number of times thus far. Most Impact Crisis referrals were good for three months, but a worker could always put in another referral after the original expired as needed. Candy made it quite clear to me that she needed Jamison out of her house, that she could not risk his hurting the other kids. As much as I liked Jamison, I totally agreed with Candy on that.

I assumed she meant to have Jamison permanently removed. Then Candy called me back and said she was going to take Jamison to St. Luke's for observation. It sounded like she couldn't make up her mind about what she wanted to do. I did note her conviction about trying to work it out with Jamison and that she had come up with several good ways to handle the situation without my or another worker's intervention. The next day, St. Luke's called Candy and asked her to pick Jamison up, but she said she couldn't do so. In the meantime we had a child family team (CFT) meeting at Jamison's school.

His new therapist led the meeting. Candy and Jonathan (the foster parents) were there. A few of Jamison's teachers attended, plus the school psychologist, the licensing agency worker, myself, the new adoptions case worker, and our supervisor, as well as Jamison's maternal grandfather, Fred. Fred had been the initial person who took Jamison in for half a year, but it got to be too much for Fred, who was starting to get up there in years.

It was our position that Jamison should remain out of the house, but Candy and Jonathan now wanted Jamison back. Jamison, in the meantime, had been sent to Canyon State Academy. I call it the military school. It was a good placement for Jamison, at least temporarily. The place was very structured. They ran a good program, and most of the kids liked it there. They also had a crisis team on hand to handle escalations. They offered therapy, an abundance of other programs, and sports of all kind. But Candy and Jonathan wanted Jamison back, and soon. That was that. A court hearing was scheduled, and the judge released Jamison back to Candy and Jonathan.

I was not sure if it was the best environment for Jamison, but you know how that goes. Whatever the judge decides, that is final. Then I got a call and email from Larry's grandma that Candy and Jonathan wouldn't let Jamison see Larry, his sibling. Roxanne and Jamison were placed together with Jonathan and Candy, but Larry went to his paternal grandmother. Our agency feels sibling contact is crucial. I emailed Lark (the paternal grandmother) to try to get once-a-month visits court ordered. I doubted the court would order it, but I couldn't think of any other suggestions at the time.

I realized that Jamison and Larry had already lost enough: their biological mother and their individual fathers. Lark also emailed me that Candy and Jonathan are not sure what to do with Jamison again. They should have thought about that before they persisted in getting him back, I thought. I knew they meant well, but still. My supervisor also commented that Grandpa Fred had said to the new supervisor (the case was transferred to an entirely new adoption unit), "Why did they even move Jamison? He was doing well at Canyon State." Exactly!

I felt like calling Fred and saying, "Good question. Go ask the judge." But I did not want to come off like a wise guy or appear disrespectful. The case ended when Jamison was removed again. I lost track of where they sent him at that point, which was after I was no longer the case worker.

Chaos, chaos, chaos. Jamison, where is the order of the universe hiding from us? Not in CPSville. Maybe in your football pass, Jamison?

36

Bobby Gonzalez

Bobby's twenty-one-year-old sister, Ariella, called in the CPS report. Bobby was in her care, though not in her legal custody. After calling the report in, the sibling called three days in a row, which were listed as status communications as opposed to CPS reports. Bobby was fourteen and did not want to listen to Ariella. He had been gotten suspended from school and was staying out until whenever he felt like it. He went in and out of the house at all hours. Bobby once broke the glass on the patio door to get in.

Ariella was a beautiful, petite girl, solemn, and very mature for her age. She had long black hair, a tiny nose, and thick, pretty lips. She was very thin, and it was hard to believe she had two little boys, ages one and three.

After we completed the investigation, I asked Ariella to call me when Bobby showed up, as he was AWOL. I would come right over. Originally I'd told Ariella to call AHIT (our after-hours team), but I had failed to send an AHIT alert, so when Bobby showed up and Ariella called AHIT, they told her to call back during the day, when I was around. I had heard of AHIT alerts but had never done one at that time, so I mistakenly thought I needed to do nothing to use their services, that AHIT would take care of whatever the situation entailed.

Anyway, when I finally spoke with Bobby, he had been out late the previous night. I went to the sister's house to find him there, still sleeping. We woke him up, and I talked with Bobby. While he did not mention disobeying his sister's rules or coming and going as he pleased, Bobby did say he was often locked out, which was why he'd busted the glass one night and why he was not doing well in school. I asked him to come with me, and Bobby did. He did not try to run or get belligerent. He came willingly.

I felt sorry for Bobby. He seemed sad instead of defiant. I called Hermina, the mom, in Tulsa and left her several messages, including information about her appearing telephonically at the TDM to decide Bobby's fate. Bobby's mom did not call; she did not show up; she did not leave me any messages trying to explain her situation. Ariella had confessed at the time of the interview that her mother had sent Bobby to Ariella without so much as asking for permission. As a matter of fact, Ariella had been in the hospital having her baby when Bobby first arrived in Phoenix. Mom did not even send with Bobby a power of attorney. Somehow Ariella had managed to get Bobby enrolled in school ten months earlier.

The good news was that his dad appeared telephonically at the TDM and said he would be happy to take Bobby. Dad had lived in Mexico since he and Mom's divorce several years earlier. Hermina infuriating me by faxing a power of attorney that allowed the adult sibling to take Bobby in and specified that Bobby should not leave the States under any circumstances.

I left Hermina a message, asking how she could dictate to us what Bobby's fate should be when she would not even appear telephonically at the TDM to discuss the reasons why he should stay as opposed to leaving. I questioned her sending the child without Ariella's consent and explained that his adult sibling called the report in to our department. Mom was one step removed, trying to control the outcome. I put in to have the case transferred; I sincerely believed Bobby should be given another shot by going to Dad's. Also, Dad should support his child if Mom wouldn't.

37

Amanda Festy

Amanda was a sixteen-year-old girl who had disclosed to her neighbors that Mom's boyfriend had taken lewd pictures of her on videotape. Apparently this had happened twice. The second time Amanda had told the neighbors. Amanda said the first time it happened, Mom just sort of brushed it off. Amanda had found evidence, unlike the first time, when the pictures had conveniently disappeared. Amanda gave the evidence to the neighbors the second time, and they'd passed it on to the police.

The police arrested the mom, Corina Mosley (at least I hope they did). Amanda's stepfather had been arrested a year earlier for committing sexual abuse against Amanda. Corina laid a guilt trip on Amanda once the police were involved, saying that now Justin wanted to commit suicide, thanks to Amanda. The minute the police detective heard that, she called me repeatedly about finding placement for Amanda. I thought the detective was going to drive me mad, and she came close to it. I told her I had an appointment to interview Corina after work. "And don't worry. I have no intention of letting Amanda go home," not to a mom like that! I would send her to a group home first if need be.

When I interviewed Corina, she seemed oblivious to the wrongdoing toward Amanda by Justin (the boyfriend) and Max, the stepdad. Her attitude was that they really were nice guys. I said that while most of us had made bad choices in our involvement with men, many women would still have the sense to put their foot down when they discovered that Max was a registered sex offender and had abused a child. Corina commented, "I trusted him." Corina seemed without emotion during the whole interview. Yet she was angry when I said she would not be allowed unsupervised visitation with her daughter. Corina sent me a look, as if her eyes had become daggers she would throw into my back. All I could hope was that the police would charge Corina and hold her accountable for her actions, or lack of them. Corina probably used Amanda as a bargaining chip with both men; for Corina to be with the men, the beautiful daughter would have to be with them as well.

Amanda wanted to stay at the neighbor's. Deedee seemed nice, but her husband, Hal, seemed loud and controlling. He kind of hovered over Amanda and cussed in front of her. When I ran their background check, I almost freaked out. They had several priors themselves involving sexual abuse going back to a time when Hal and Deedee weren't married. It sounded like Hal's son and Deedee's daughter got into a sexual relationship of sorts.

Hal's son was registered as a sex offender, and Deedee's daughter left Arizona to live with her dad. However, it sounded like the Albertsons had sided with Hal's son during the whole incident, who wasn't a minor at the time, though Deedee's daughter was. Also, Hal had hit Deedee's daughter and left marks. They weren't going to work out as safety monitors. The Albertsons lived near Amanda and her mom in a place called New River, near Anthem. I was starting to wonder what kind of people lived in New River.

I ignored how floored Hal was at the TDM when he learned that Amanda was going to go home with her father. It was true that father and daughter had had a somewhat shaky relationship in the past, but we hoped all that would change with our services. Jason, the dad, admitted he had been a drug user until three years ago. He'd had a temper in the past, but he was not going to endanger his child. I felt he was appropriate but lacked confidence in himself. I was hoping that maybe with time he would get that back. At least he was able and willing to provide for his child. At the time, it seemed like maybe nobody was happy, but the child was safe. And maybe father and daughter could salvage their relationship.

38

Helena Cisorsk and Other CPS-Related Ponderings

CPS was called on Helena because she was in a near-fatal car crash after taking too many prescription meds. She claimed she took them on an empty stomach because she was depressed and didn't feel like eating. Luckily, her one-month-old baby was not in the car with her at the time of the accident. When the police were called, the dad had the baby in his custody. Then Mom got out of the hospital and called the police because she wanted her baby back. That was when I entered the picture.

So there was Mom, frantic to get the baby back. While Dad did let Mom see the baby every day, he did not leave her alone with the baby. That was responsible of him. It was also required of him, as there was a safety plan already put in place by AHIT (the after-hours team) when the accident occurred. Mom was living in a nice house at the time, but her house was being foreclosed on. It was in Anthem, near Tramonte. I had looked at houses there before I bought and lost my house in Peoria. Beautiful Helena was a model, but she told me she had been unable to model the last few months of her pregnancy.

Helena had met Joseph, the dad, a few years earlier. I asked how they met, and Helena said from mutual friends. I later wondered about that, as Joseph was a well-to-do financial banker living in Fountain Hills. I would have thought they had different social circles, but perhaps not. Helena told me she had earned an economics degree from a college in Bulgaria, her homeland. If that were the case, I suppose it was possible the two of them met in financial circles.

In any case, Helena's place was beautifully furnished. Helena was not only a very pretty girl in her late twenties, she dressed to the hilt, the way a professional model would. She was very thin for a five-foot-nine woman who had had a baby one month previously. I wandered about that part too. Helena told me she had gained a healthy thirty pounds during the pregnancy. Her medical records stated she weighed 120 two weeks earlier. How could a normal person possibly lose twenty-plus pounds in two weeks. That did not make sense to me.

I thought I had noticed in her medical records a diagnosis of anorexia. Did that explain it? There was also a comment about "Helena having control over her body," but I doubted that. Between overmedicating and her other issues, I don't think she had control over anything.

Helena had told me at the interview that she'd lived in Arizona for five years. She had also lived in several other states: Delaware, Pennsylvania—I forget the rest. She was just now going through a divorce. She'd experienced domestic violence with the guy she had married. To top it, at the beginning of the end, Helena had found out her husband had cheated on her. Helena claimed her husband wanted a baby, but she couldn't get pregnant. Listening to Helena, I did not feel she offered much stability.

Then she met Joseph. Helena went with Joseph for a while, got pregnant, miscarried, got pregnant again and had an abortion. They broke up. Then they got back together, and Helena got pregnant again. This time Helena was determined to have the baby, no matter what, although Helena alleged that Joseph wanted nothing to do with the pregnancy. Later Joseph would say that the whole time he knew Helena, she had mental health issues that never seemed to be resolved. (That seemed very believable.) So his point of view was that he cared about Helena but was leery of her and of her having a baby. If it weren't for all her issues, he would have been happy to get married and share a life.

Joseph expressed hopes that he could help Helena become stable, so that she could share joint custody. He felt a child shouldn't be taken from his mother. Yet he felt it was necessary to protect the child. This seemed like a reasonable and appropriate attitude. I could not fault Joseph for trying to be levelheaded—somebody had to be. Emotionally, Helena was out of control.

She minimized CPS's concerns about her actions, which led to our involvement. Helena's whole focus seemed to center on how Joseph had done her wrong, not the safety of the baby. A lot of people confuse CPS with custody court. We don't decide who the best parent is; we are involved to ensure the child is safe in his or her home. Custody court can address who is the most qualified person to raise the child or decide about joint custody and other related issues when a dependency is not filed or is dismissed.

Anyway, at the TDM, Mom denied she had become violent toward Joseph. It was one person's word against the other. However, Helena's records indicated possible mental health issues, in addition to the original near-fatal accident. It was decided at the TDM, therefore, that Joseph should continue to keep the baby for the time being and that Mom would need to do services. After she completed the services, it custody court could then determine the best option regarding joint or sole custody.

I put in the referrals. One was for Family Preservation (FPPT), an intensive service that worked with both parents in their homes, usually three times a week. I put in for a psychological evaluation for Mom, which would take a while to get done, The request went through our district office, and they take the referrals in the order they are received. Unless they are totally swamped, it usually took thirty days to assign to a provider, but it could be closer to sixty days when they were very busy. (Unless they lose your referral. Then you have to wait even longer.)

I also put in a referral for the TERROS drug program for Helena. While prescription drugs are classified differently than the illegal ones, if someone misuses his or her prescription/s, that would definitely need to be addressed. Maybe there's a difference between the two, but both can kill when someone overdoses. In Helena's case, maybe the reason she went to several different doctors was so that she had a good variety in her stash.

Helena called me as much as ten times a day. I explained the service providers would be calling her; she would need to work with them. I also gave Joseph and Helena custody court info, including the phone number and address. Helena said she would wait until she did the services before going to court, to show the court she "wasn't crazy."

Helena called me one day and admitted she lied at the TDM. She had gotten physical with Joseph. She was frustrated at not having the baby and said that "Joseph was so cold to her." I appreciated her honesty and told her so.

Helena believed that Joseph had an attachment disorder because he was adopted, and that could be an influence. I never delved into whether he was adopted or not with Joseph. He seemed to have great interactions with his son. And he stated he had family who helped him with the baby, his mom and sis.

Helena said she had been afraid to mention the domestic violence at the TDM, because she thought it would be used against her. I agreed and thought to myself, *This is another issue that factors into the equation.* Plus she had experienced DV previously with her husband. She was establishing a history of domestic violence by her own admission.

Helena blamed a lot of her state of mind on Joseph's treatment of her, but, in addition, the baby had a medical condition. The baby was a tad shorter on one side than the other. I told Helena my chiropractor said the same thing of me and that it was not a big deal. Many people are shorter on one side than the other. Helena made the baby sound like he was deformed. It wasn't really even noticeable. When I interviewed Joseph, I also saw the baby.

I know Mom was anguished about little Nate. I can understand feeling bad but not to the extent of falling apart over it. Perhaps Helena's most significant unstable factor surfaced over the summer of 2007. At that time she was pregnant. She text-messaged Joseph that she was going to kill herself and the baby. Joseph showed me the text messages on his cell phone. I remember saying to Helena that sending the text messages was not a wise thing to do. She claimed she did it to try to get Joseph's attention.

I told Helena that CPS could not discount that threat as if it meant nothing. One of the problems with CPS, especially if mental health issues are involved, is that it's hard to distinguish when a person might be saying something just to be manipulative from when the person is going to act on their words. What if the person were to commit the act later?

Could you imagine being the case worker standing there, with television cameras surrounding you, saying, "Well, she gave me her word she wasn't going to kill herself and the child, even though she originally threatened she would." In short, we can't disregard the fact a threat has been made, no matter what the motivation or intention. The same applies to the kids and teens. If they threaten to take their lives, we have to take it seriously. Even if not meant seriously, we would have to question what was making that child say something so drastic. On the other hand, you can be trained in social work, psychology, or CPS, but nobody has a crystal ball to see the future or what lies deep in someone's heart that moves the person to action. People do snap—all the time.

You might go on an investigation where everything looks stable and safe. Who's to say that a new drug user couldn't become overly zealous while effectively controlling his newfound habit for a short while, then go out, get methed out, and hear hallucinations "from God" telling him to sacrifice that child, or some such crazy nonsense. If you think this is farfetched, know that in class, we have watched real cases of meth users who went off the deep end and committed murder. One guy lovingly took his son to McDonald's and then a few hours later got too high and chopped up the kid's body in the desert.

Nothing in life is 100 percent foolproof. This book is not to make excuses for CPS or sway you that one shouldn't hold CPS accountable if a child dies but to make you aware that sometimes it is close to impossible to predict child abuse while it's unfolding. A new drug user or someone with mental health issues can present as perfectly functional just one moment before the person is suddenly much worse; the situation escalates to an extreme in the next moment. Some things are just not foreseeable.

It is similar to the medical profession, I think. Sometimes a doctor treats a patient, offers a diagnosis, or operates. Sometimes the treatment, diagnosis, or operation is successful, but once in a while it isn't, even if it should be. An operation could be successful with one individual but not another, maybe because that person's immunity is weaker. Maybe the person forgot to mention other symptoms or medications or other factors that come into play. Sometimes something went unexpectedly wrong when the probability of it going wrong was small, but it happened nonetheless.

One thing is for sure: if it involves a child, people will point their finger at CPS before they will at the parent. Why? Because a child dying or getting into a horrible predicament is a tragedy, and denial is easier than facing facts. Emotions become overly heated. Sometimes people involved don't want to be held accountable for their actions. With CPS, it is a job, and we are supposed to get the job done. So it is easier to blame CPS.

If I see someone as much as leave a mark on a child, I tell the person it is against the law in Arizona. If the police have not been called, we notify the police ourselves. Back in the '70s, when removal of children was alleged to be more commonplace, statistics showed removal does not help kids. Too often, the trauma made criminals of those kids when they grew up. I think the reason was lack of attachment. That is why social work evolved the way it did: let us get in there, assess the situation, and provide services to deal with the major issues.

These services were designed to make the family unit stronger so it might function on its own and children would be safer in their environment. For a large family, even if they had food stamps, the supplemental food boxes could make a significant difference. We tried to identify these areas of concern to help solve the problem that led to our involvement. We hoped our help would create a more peaceful and less stressful home life for the child.

Some parents were so wrapped up in their own situations that they ignored or neglected the needs of the children, or their fears. Some parents would ridicule their kids to the point where the child might want to hurt himself. Some of the parents hated the child because the child reminded them too much of the ex, whom they now hated and wanted revenge against. Some parents would use their kids as bargaining chips, a means of negotiation to get what they wanted, like Rita did with her daughter in a previous chapter.

How did I know if that was what Helena had in mind when she got pregnant? After all, didn't Helena move in with Joseph at some stage of her pregnancy? And wasn't moving to that home in Fountain Hills a big trade up from her townhouse? Yes, she had a nice place, but Joseph's place was much bigger, with a much nicer view and more status. And Helena seemed very swayed by status. Helena said Joseph was cheap, that she had been the one to buy all the stuff for the baby. She also said that when her car broke down and she asked to borrow one of Joseph's three cars, he told her no. Still, Joseph was not the out-of-control parent, even if he could have been more generous to Helena. Maybe he was afraid she would crash his car; she'd totaled her own.

There is an interesting related phenomenon when we find parents are only into the kid and not into the other parent. It can be as if the other parent is only the means to an end (to have a child), as if they are a mating device. What is that parent teaching his or her kid about relationships: that relationships don't matter or aren't valuable? It teaches a kid not about love but maybe about manipulation, not about involvement but about lack of attachment. I was wondering if Helena fit this description, considering her status-seeking tendencies.

CPS kids: they're either last on the attention list or they're overly exposed to it. They live with extremes compared to the rest of us, who reside with a sense of normalcy. I notice that most CPS parents tend to be unmarried and probably don't value their partner or ex to any great degree. They could move in with their next partner without taking adequate time to get to know the person. Maybe it is elements like these which feed the growth of neglect and abuse among children. Those children grow up with contempt and anger. While children are very resilient, they all thrive on consistency. And after all, old habits die hard.

39

Courtney Blockis

Courtney seemed strange, though it was difficult to pinpoint exactly how. Maybe because Courtney, while articulate, rambled, to the extent it was next to impossible to follow her train of thought. (In my worse moments, I have probably exhibited a similar tendency.) Everyone who encountered Courtney felt this way about her. To add to it, she seemed very snide, which made conversing with her annoying and hard. She was way up there on the list of people who rubbed me the wrong way. She might have been at the top of the list, as a matter of fact. I tried to not let that get in the way, because I did want to do my job properly by remaining unbiased. It was a challenge sometimes to remain unbiased.

The reason for the CPS report was that Courtney's daughter, Tamara, had horrible school attendance, and sometimes Mom would pick Tamara up hours after school had let out. Also, it was reported by the school that various strange men would pick up the child as well. When I was assigned the report that day, it was the fill-in supervisor (my regular supervisor was out with the flu) who advised me that the dad of the sibling probably had called the report in. Actually, it was the school. In the prior investigation the dad of the sibling had called it in.

My assessment was quite a bit different than my coworker's. While the house was meticulous, beautifully furnished and well kept, and the child did seem healthy and unafraid of her mom, nonetheless, the mother's attitude filled me with alarm. When I brought up the topic of the child's attendance, the mother seemed unconcerned. When I asked her, "Don't you want your daughter to do well in life?" she became very sarcastic and hostile. "What do you think? Of course I do! Do you think I want her to have a lousy life?" Her tone of voice was downright rude; I was only asking her a question born of concern. I worried that she talked with her child in that tone of voice.

When I asked why Courtney was making it hard on Tamara by allowing her to miss so much school, her reply was totally off the wall. "I got beat for getting A-minuses when I was in school, and where did it get me?" I could not connect to the point she was making, which made me worry if perhaps Courtney had mental health issues. When I asked if there was enough food in the house, Courtney replied, "I can show you. Can't you tell Tamara eats well? She's like twenty pounds overweight." Tamara was actually average, so again I was upset with Mom's blunt, bordering on mean answer and her perception.

This went on for a while, until I came to the conclusion that Courtney either had mental health issues or was on drugs, or possibly both. Courtney was bone thin. I later found out from Daniel, the dad, that Courtney had lost a lot of weight and aged ten years over the last year or so. Courtney complained of being broke, and that was why Daniel had custody of their child. I asked if Courtney worked. She said she had three jobs: interior designing (which was believable, judging from her place), doing taxes, and financial planning. I remarked she must be doing well, and she divulged that her house was being foreclosed on.

Courtney's monthly expenses were supposedly $5,000. She paid $50,000 to fight her boyfriend for custody of her son, which she lost. When a person cannot live within his or her means, it courts disaster, but I felt somehow she was exaggerating.

I previously mentioned that I lost my house. I moved in with someone and based the expenses on both incomes. But when that fell through, I had enough sense of responsibility and foresight to plan how not tobe foreclosed on. I moved on without losing everything.

I went to visit Courtney and Daniel's son, and his interview told me a lot. Little Mason was glad he was living with his dad because "Mom did not have a car. Also a bunch of strange men come and go at her house." I asked Mason if he knew if Mom did drugs. He said he didn't know but added that they "smoked smelly cigarettes." Well, at least she had the decency to cover up for the most part if she was using drugs.

Because Mom refused services and had such a combative attitude, I informed the school that if Tamara were to continue missing school, the resource officer at the school could take Mom to court and hold her liable. However, I did not feel we had enough on Courtney to take custody of Tamara. At least not yet.

My supervisor instructed me to put in for services anyway. When I called Courtney, her call blocking disconnected us automatically. I called Daniel; he laughed about it. He said he would keep his eye on things. That was the best we could do for the moment. For all it's worth, at least I didn't receive another report on the family.

40

Ava Mastroni

I did investigations for three or so years and spent seven years in an ongoing unit. An ongoing unit is involved when a child has to be removed from home but the parent is trying to go through the legal system in order to get the child back into their custody. In the seven years I worked in ongoing, I regret to say I was only able to reunify a handful of children with their parents. Services are provided that help the parents try to reunify.

Ava, one of my ongoing cases, was from a very respectable middle-class African American family. Ava had mental health issues. As hard as it could be for parents to get off drugs, some losing their rights instead of losing the drugs, in some instances a parent with mental health issues can be a more difficult challenge than someone considered strung out. Such was Ava.

Our agency provided a parent aide to assist Ava. (The parent aide actually helped Mom to interact with her child and discipline him. Previously, Ava just sat there, spaced out, looking off in the distance while her son entertained himself.) Ava was also given a psychological evaluation, which recommended counseling. No shock there. Did I fail to mention the reason for Carl's removal? Ava heard voices saying that someone was raping her six-year-old son. Ava's own brother was one of the "suspects," as well as the Mesa Police Department. (She called Mesa PD to report the sexual abuse and "heard her son in the background, and that was how she knew the Mesa PD was in on it.")

Ava was supposed to be on meds and usually was. But if she went out with friends (which happened on a weekly basis), she felt she had to have a drink. Her rationalization was "If I have a drink, I cannot mix a drink and my meds. If I do mix the two, I still hear voices. I hear voices even when I take my meds and don't have drinks." (Everyone in this field has their unique rationalizations, and Ava was right up there with the rest of them.) The son, Carl, was intelligent and loving. He enjoyed his visits with his mom but refused to call her Mom. Carl called Mom by her first name, Ava, and called his maternal aunt Mommy. He somehow sensed at age six that his mom was off kilter. He did not want to identify her as Mom, even though he was told she was his mom.

The dad was in prison. Ava had an inappropriate boyfriend who could not pass a background check. Ava had to live with a relative, as she was unable to hold a job. She wasn't capable of handling the types of responsibilities that a normally functioning adult would need to handle in order to be reunified with their child.

At the trial, my attorney used good strategy and cut to the chase. She asked Ava if Ava was still on meds, to which Ava replied yes. My attorney then asked if she still heard voices. Ava smiled and replied yes, she still heard voices, whether she took her meds or not. Mom's rights were severed. The case went to the adoptions unit. Adorable Carl, who was thriving very well with his auntie, whom he called Mom, was provided the chance to grow up in a nice, stable, very sane home environment.

41

Vanessa Valenzula

Vanessa Valenzula was a Hispanic woman with minimal education. She had a nice, respectable extended family but seemed to have little going for her and did not appear motivated to change her living circumstances. Vanessa had two very tiny, smiley-faced dark-haired children, one and two years old. The two-year-old was a female, Sandy, and the one-year-old was a little boy named Corey. Sandy and Corey had a close relationship with each other. Sandy tried to baby her little brother.

Vanessa loved meth more than her children. She was also a gang member. The children's dad was in prison for drugs and gang-related activities. Vanessa had another boyfriend at the time the children were removed. Vanessa used all of the meth belonging to one of the gang members, and, when confronted, she told the individual that her boyfriend had done the drugs instead of admitting she had done them. Consequently, the individual shot her boyfriend in the head, and Vanessa took off running, leaving the two kids there at the scene of the crime. Miraculously, the boyfriend lived, and the gang member whose drugs Vanessa stole did not shoot the two children.

During all of this, Dad was released from prison. Mom and Dad came to my Tempe CPS Office (I worked first at Glendale, then Thunderbird, then Tempe, then Mesa during my ten years of service), hell bent on getting their children back. They were never able to make the appropriate behavioral changes in order to remedy the reason for the children's removal. So that meant another severance. And then another baby came.

Bottom line: some moms keep having babies whether they are able to care for them or not.

42

Karen Brown

Karen Brown was a thin, blonde female who was a self-proclaimed Messiah. She used prostitution and witchcraft as part of her religion. Karen used quite a few drugs, mostly meth, on a regular basis. She would invite men over and have sex with them in one room while her daughter Ariana, a petite eight-year-old version of her mom, was in the room next door. Ariana's "bible" was a book of spells that Karen had given her. I took this "bible" away from Ariana, it being inappropriate reading material for a little girl. Ariana never argued or asked for the book. It seemed like Mom had imposed those "lessons" on Ariana and that Ariana was confused by their contents.

I asked Karen one day if she were able to put aside her religious beliefs in order to reunify with her child, and she hesitated. I guess one could say that Karen had both mental health and drug issues.

Mom told Ariana her pets had been run over while Ariana was in foster care. Ariana cried and cried. I felt bad for this poor, heartbroken child who so loved her pets. I decided to go to Karen's house unannounced one day and saw both pets were alive and well. I told Ariana as much.

At some point I was able to locate Ariana's dad, who lived in Montana. The father had custody of Ariana at the time that Karen absconded with Ariana. Dad then moved to Arizona for six months so that he could go through the reunification process with Ariana. Before Ariana left with her dad to return to Montana permanently, Ariana showed me a picture she drew that explained her history. In the picture, Ariana is holding Mom's hand but trying to reach her dad's hand; Dad's hand is held out toward Ariana. They both had big smiles on their face as they reached out for each other.

Although Ariana had a bedwetting problem during the length of the dependency, it stopped the minute she was returned to Dad's custody. This case had a rare happy ending.

43

Josey Montana

Josey Montana had a cute little boy, David, age nine, with black hair and a whimsical smile. He was an average build and liked what most kids his age liked. Josey's drug of choice was OxyContin, and she had been a heavy user for a long time. At the time of David' removal, her current boyfriend, Andy, was chasing David around the swimming pool, trying to pull down his swimming suit. David was very upset about this and told his grandma, whom Josey was living with at the time.

Grandma was angry and called in a CPS report. Grandma did not approve of Josey's drug use, associates, or life style or her upbringing of David. David's dad had not been involved in the picture for a long time.

During the course of the dependency, Josey got back with her other boyfriend, Isaac. Isaac came across as very strange, even though on the surface he was a successful businessman. He proclaimed himself to be David's "psychological father," which piqued my suspicions. I could not figure out what a successful, nondrug user who earned a lot of money, a well-dressed yuppie type, would see in a woman who was strung out on downers and spacey, who did not display common sense or stability and started every sentence with the word *like*. She would say, "Like when it happened, like all I could think of was, like ..." She spoke very slowly, constantly lose her train of thought, if she had one.

Josey had totaled three cars that Isaac bought her; each time she totaled a car, he bought her another one! (Although I hear the last one he bought her was used, not new like the other two cars.) During the duration of the case, Mom was provided with a parent aide who supervised the visit and made suggestions related to Josey's parenting skills. These reports were disclosed to the court. In addition, Josey was required to do a drug program and drug testing. She wound up going to an expensive, private methadone clinic, where her dosage levels kept increasing. I did not consider this encouraging by any means. If a person is trying to get off drugs, no matter what they are, the person should strive to decrease the levels of usage, not increase them.

In the meantime, in one of the parent aide reports, David told his mom Isaac made him wear a dress because all his clothes were in the dirty wash. What did Mom do? She changed the subject quickly! Well, I was livid when I read that. Then I started to look at the bigger picture: Isaac took David to Europe alone a few years before, when David was six. I recalled how awkward their interaction was at the visit Isaac attended with David. They did not look bonded at all. I was certain that Isaac was trying to "groom" David, that he was a sexual predator looking for a target. Isaac knew he could keep Josey at bay with the proper amount of drugs, which he always gave her the money for if she could not get them legally.

At the severance trial, Isaac used an interesting strategy. Since Josey could not keep a job or her finances together, in addition to her drug problem, Isaac married Josey to provide financial security for she and David. He hired her an excellent private attorney instead of letting the court appoint her one. Luckily, it made no difference. When asked at trial what date she and Isaac got married, Josey did not know. Obviously the marriage was not built on love and commitment.

The charade was transparent: Josey's rights were severed, and David was adopted by his maternal aunt, a kind Mormon woman with good values who was very caring with her vulnerable nephew.

44

Another Baby Who Died

A coworker had a case of a baby who died. I don't remember the exact age of the baby, but the child was probably around three or four months. The pictures of the infant told the whole story. The baby started out healthy: chubby, with glowing pink cheeks, nice smooth skin, and sparkling eyes. When you compared pictures of the infant just prior to the time of death, it looked like a holocaust infant. The child's skin stretched across its fragile frame; ribs protruded. The face was all bone, the eyes dull and sorrowful. The stretched but wrinkly skin gave the infant a hard-core look, like an old person in a tiny body.

Here is the horrible story/truth behind the death. The mom had apparent mental health issues. Depressed after having her third child, she stopped feeding the baby or fed the infant too little for the child to thrive. The dad was a long-distance truck driver. While he did go home periodically, he was away much of the time. (You mean to tell me this guy was so robotic or unobservant that he didn't notice his little girl whittling away, struggling to stay alive?) When my friend Brenda did the investigation, she noticed a pantry full of formula. That was part of the tragedy. The food was "within reach" but not a baby's reach. Neither the eighteen-month-old or the just-turned three sibling could reach or prepare it for their sibling. CPS workers are taught that the most vulnerable ages for child abuse center around children age up to five years old.

The two well-fed siblings were removed from the home and were placed with relatives. Thank God for relatives who are able to step in, but where were they while the baby was being starved to death? (I believe they lived in Arizona but were not close to the family. Unfortunately, nobody had stopped over to visit, which might have prevented the death.) I don't know if the parents were charged with child abuse, but I hope so. I do know it was Brenda's last case. She quit and went back to nursing school. She was pregnant at the time and took the death very hard, maybe harder than the parents did.

It was one of the worse cases I knew of. I had been there a year and a half at the time. Another was Victoria's case one or two years ago. The father killed his two-year-old; the evidence was in the text messages from Dad to Mom, trying to cover the murder. Mom had failed to protect, allowing the father to murder the child and then trying to help him with his alibi. Was the truck driver father who let the infant starve any better? Victoria's murder case happened when I had been working at my job for eight and a half years.

Isn't it a wonder I made it to ten years at the job? (And isn't it understandable why the average worker will last a year, regardless of age, experience, and background, despite the workload, with all the nightmares of the job to contend with and the nightmare of the CPS parents they usually deal with, so forlorn and deficit.) ?)

45

Conclusion

When a person looks at CPS statistics, many areas are bleak. Let's consider the turnover rate. When I worked at Glendale, they had approximately twenty investigators. I was there for approximately a year and a half. By the time I transferred to Thunderbird, there were only three other people still in investigations from when I'd first started. One had been there for three years; the other two had been there as long as I had. The stress of the job is enormous, partially because of the volume of work and partially because there are nonstop crisis situations to be dealt with on a regular and constant basis. I venture to guess that working for CPS is parallel to being a police officer.

And while no CPS workers have been killed in the greater Phoenix area, there was a case of a volunteer who went to deliver a food box and wound up dead after being raped and dismembered. Yes, it was a methed-up father who did this poor churchgoing woman the "honors" right in front of his children. Most severance cases involve the use of methamphetamines.

The few that were not drug cases were mental health issues, whether officially diagnosed or not. In the cases with diagnoses, the parents denied that they had mental health issues and would not take their meds. "I'm not crazy" is the most predictable response, allowing the dysfunctional person to continue to operate, to everybody's dismay, especially the children's. Usually the most violent cases were the mental health and meth cases. The meth moms who were using would party and put the drugs and boyfriends before the needs of their kids.

It seems quite a few CPS parents basically grew up underprivileged and without good educations; they usually had the most kids (the more kids, the more the moms couldn't handle them). Often the worst cases involved single moms without a good support system. I don't know if it was a generalized lack of commitment that invited CPS in or their own sordid pasts taking root and perpetuating. If the grandparents were recovered drug addicts, they could not pass a background check to be considered as a foster placement for most practical purposes.

I began to ask quite a number of kids what they wanted out of life. I tried to encourage them to focus on school, assuring them that they could grow up to be somebody special and live a good life instead of struggling their entire lives. I figured I could try to plant seeds of hope so discouragement wasn't their only companion.

I thought back to my own life, my own past. I wish I'd found someone with more in common to share a life with than my ex. No wonder we wound up divorced. If I had found someone more suited to my background, maybe I would have been much better off, instead of alone and always working so many hours. Social circles are important. I worked a good part of my life away, close to my parents for the most part, but I could have maintained much stronger social ties to my cultural community if I had stayed closer to it. To wind up single and working many hours was alienating.

Maybe in retirement I will achieve what I should have strived for earlier. Though I used to be quite a free spirit, I see now that the institutions of religion and marriage should never be underrated. I have seen that the happiest people are loving parents who raise a family and shower love and attention as they back each other. When a person is divorced or single, the kid/s get gypped, as my own sweet son did. Yes, families may have problems, but solving them as a unit is better than doing so alone.

There is a balance between what a mother can provide and what a father can provide. I am relieved and happy to say that my son has good values. Maybe the hard efforts put forth by my ex and I did pay off. But I think if we had had more similar values and had lived as a harmonious couple together, my son would have had an easier time socializing. What he has internalized does worry me. And it's almost too late to go back and undo what damage was done in the long separation between me and my ex. The hurt remains; I am sure of that.

CPS has taught me a lot. My cases sometimes showed me where I went wrong in my own life. Maybe that was why I was so compassionate—because I did see that discrepancy within me. I even wonder why I didn't get therapy for Dan and me to help deal with issues about his dad and me. Or, better yet, get the therapy before we split up? Hindsight is a funny thing. You can look back and see clearly what the right course of action to take would have been. That is not unlike the analogy of going from being a kid to an adult. Or did it just take me a lot longer to grow up, having lived the indulged lifestyle I did as a youth? (Since I was from a middle-class environment, I never wanted for anything and never dwelled on how to strategize and earn certain things in life because they were there for the taking. Some disadvantaged children grow up much quicker than yours truly.)

In any case, I try to bring that wisdom with me when I go out on my cases. I had a strange case a few years ago with a girl named Sonjee. It was sad too. Her mom had been in a car accident seventeen years earlier with her infant brother. The sibling died. Sonjee was fifteen when I met her; she was not born at the time of Mom's accident. Apparently, Mom was drunk when it happened. Fast forward to a few years ago: Mom went to the store and was drunk. She did not take Sonjee with her that time, though she always did otherwise. Sonjee was freaking out. She'd had a dream the night before the incident that Mom was going to die. And Mom did die. But at least Sonjee was not with her, unlike her sibling who had passed away in the car with Mom years ago. We have cycles, and we have fate. Sonjee and her family were examples of when cycles of fate were obvious and distinct.

I like to say to my son, " I am sorry for the times I let you down, no matter what the reason. I love you, and you have always deserved better than I could give you. I wish you a meaningful life in a relationship with someone who loves you and whom you love. I wish you more family unity instead of less; more family get-togethers on both sides, not just one side; more understanding of cultural and social circles for you to be a part of instead of standing alone too much; greater resources for activities that might not have been available to you previously; more hugs and kisses and more I love yous from me, if you'll let me; more encouragement, attention, and time."

Time is the greatest commodity of all, one which we too often squander on things of lesser importance than those we love.

89626356R00107

Made in the USA
Lexington, KY
31 May 2018